FOREWORD

2006, London Design Week: two people lean over an elegant white table playing a new-age version of the classic 70's Atari Pong game, the track pads and ball made up of touch sensitive, sunset-orange LEDs, glowing through the Corian® surface. Witty, humorous, retro but futuristic, I was determined to meet the man behind the table, Moritz Waldemeyer. Since then curiosity led me to follow each of his projects, from Yves Behar's Voyage Chandelier to Zaha Hadid's Z Island Kitchen. I was intrigued as to how they each worked. A year later, we met in Milan and Moritz explained everything that he does and can do. It was fascinating. I knew I wanted us to work together.

Moritz has been at the top of my list for many years. Of course I could have brought some pieces to exhibit in Japan at any point, but that was not the sort of project I wanted. In 2012, five years after I founded my publishing house, Clear Edition, the perfect venture emerged. I believe that artist's books are precious collectibles for everyone, yet my aim beyond this is to develop new ideas for new markets. Moritz's name has made an impression in surprising areas - the fashion industry, the music industry, and the architectural industry, rather than pure product design. His experiments have grown, catching different audiences, one by one. I wish to spur this on.

This book shows the nature of Moritz's ideas, full of experimentation, trial and error, and open to new directions. Lighting is Moritz's speciality but he is not a lighting designer. The spirit of his work provokes emotions of surprise, transfixion and bliss. Moritz wants us to share the awe-inspiring feeling when you gaze at the stars on a clear night.

January 2013
Yoichi Nakamuta,
Founder
Clear Edition & Gallery

INTROD

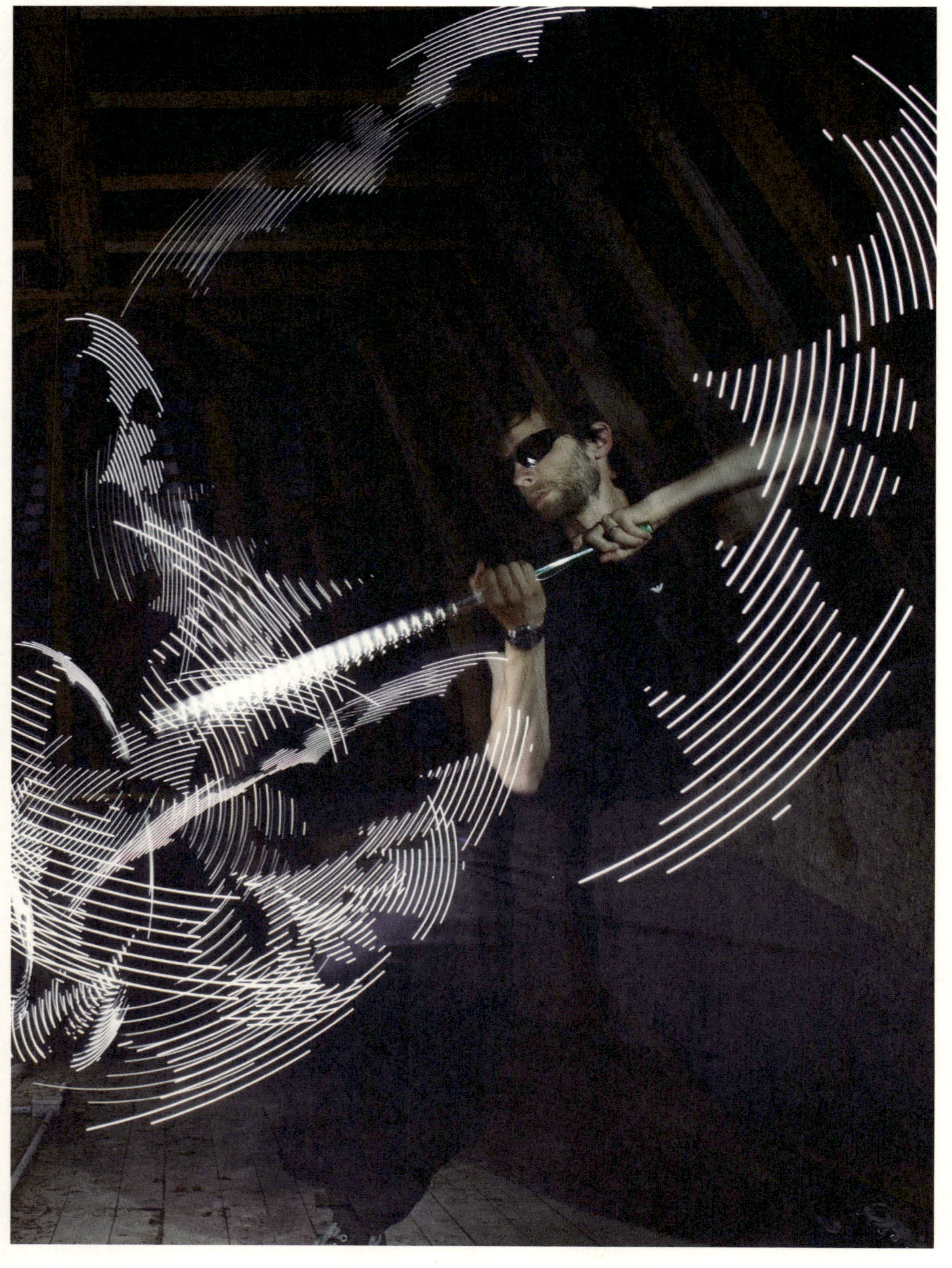

'The Path of the Sword' charts the journey from rough experimental photographs of LED installations to a formal exploration of painting with light. Over the past decade, LED mechatronics maestro, Moritz Waldemeyer, has collected photographs of his collaborations with some of the best-known names in design; Zaha Hadid, Yves Behar and Fredrikson Stallard. Each chandelier, or installation takes on an entirely new form - abstract and ephemeral - when photographed under long exposure. From this, the project was born. Moritz began to question the potential of using LEDs as moving artwork:

JCTION

"I GREW UP IN A FAMILY OF ARTISTS SO ART WAS NOT FOREIGN TO ME, IT JUST TOOK ME A WHILE TO REALISE THAT I WANTED TO DO THAT TOO. FOR ME, LIGHT IS THE MATERIAL WITH WHICH I WORK. JUST LIKE A PAINTER WHO WORKS WITH PAINT AND CANVASES, I WORK WITH ELECTRONICS, LEDS AND LIGHT."

The notion of painting with light is familiar from childhood, when using sparklers to spell out a word or draw a flower. Moritz Waldemeyer takes the phenomenon of persistence of vision into the 21st Century, exploring how modern materials – computer programmed LEDs – can produce new effects.

Moritz principally engages with the concept through the agility and aestheticism of martial arts. This marrying of ideas is not coincidental – the relationship between calligraphy and martial arts, brush and sword, runs deep through Chinese culture: for centuries the two have gone hand in hand in the training of warriors, who have incorporated aesthetic concepts and philosophy into their practice. Such harmonious movements of body and weapon inspired Moritz's collaboration with some of the UK's finest practitioners. The project is a means of visualising the poetry of their moves and applying a stream of graphics to them, embodying brush and sword simultaneously.

This book frames Moritz's two collaborations with martial artists in the context of the initial inspiration for the project, the experiments undertaken during two workshops on the subject, further projects inspired by the results, and finally, the video for Ellie Goulding's single 'Lights'. The Ellie Goulding video stills showcase the spontaneity and elegance of the medium when expressed through minimalist dance. Using a sword-like LED-embellished prop inspires dynamic, combative moves reminiscent of martial arts but paired down. This subtlety perfectly complements the LED graphics and marks the culmination of Moritz exploration into painting with light.

INTRODUCTION AND TEXT BY FLORENCE GRAHAM-DIXON

FOR SILVIA, ELETTRA AND LEONARDO

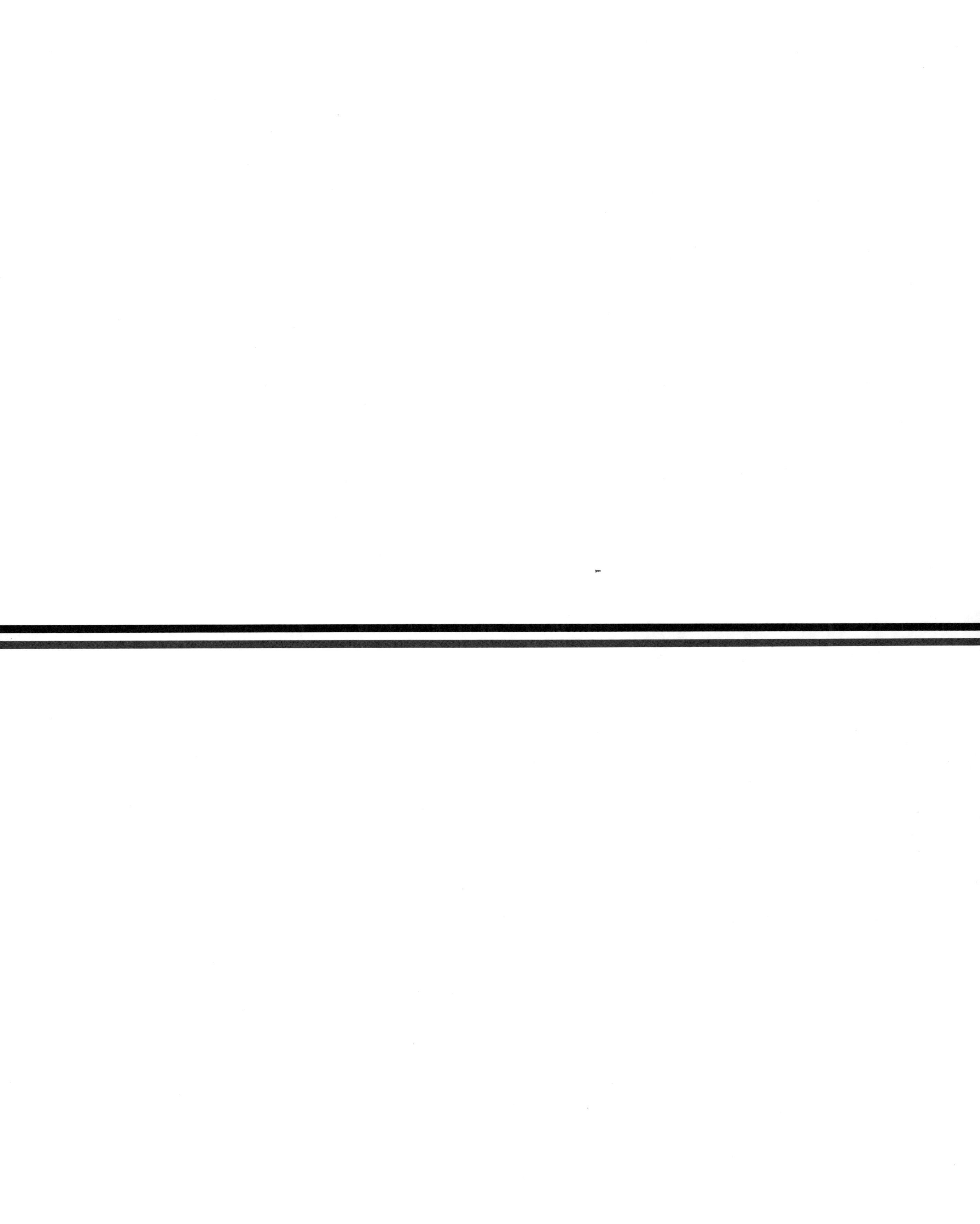

SHOW ME THE LIG

In these few abstract shots of installations that Moritz Waldemeyer collaborated on, we see this project in embryo:

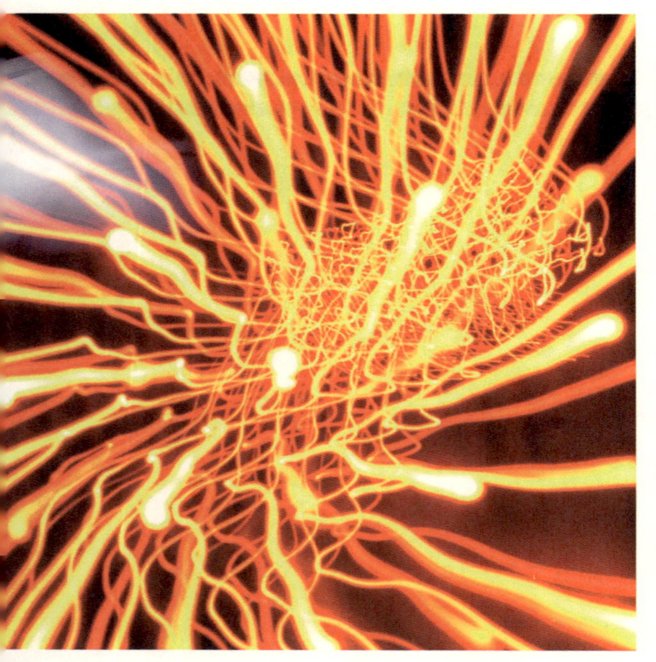

"I WAS STRUCK BY HOW THESE RECOGNISABLE PROJECTS FROM THE DESIGN WORLD TAKE ON AN ENTIRELY NEW LIFE. THEY ARE TRANSFORMED INTO MESMERIZING, SPONTANEOUS, ABSTRACT FORMS – AS IF EACH LED OF THE ORIGINAL INSTALLATION WERE A LOADED PAINTBRUSH AND THE CAMERA FILM A CANVAS THAT YOU COULD WHISK ALONG THEM."

It is precisely this idea - LEDs as loaded paintbrushes – that is at the heart of the concept. Its versatility is clear from the distinct aura of each of these early shots, shown on the next few pages: one Zaha Hadid prototype takes on the organic quality of the inside of a seashell, another suggests the form of iridescent, snake-like plankton, while various other prototypes seem almost to twist light into various geometric whirlpools of vibrant colour. The most figurative of the collection, Fredrikson Stallard's Pandora chandelier, (designed for Swarovski Crystal Palace) is given movement, as if it has swung down from the heavens. The kaleidoscopic colour is created by the refraction of natural light in the Swarovski crystals. The camera, held still on the chandelier and then pulled away, reveals workings of the materials that are invisible to the naked eye. The swirl of text is achieved by waving the camera past a Jenny Holzer text-inscribed component of a Philippe Starck lamp.

HT

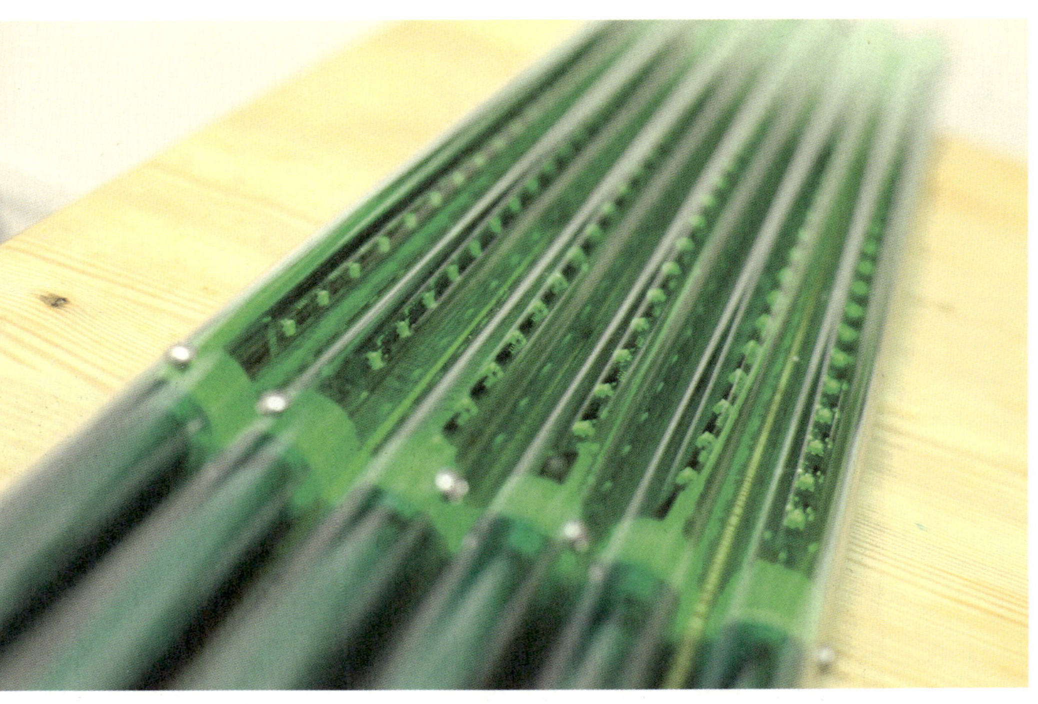

These images take the focus away from the object and towards the potential of the technology itself, expressed through the medium of long-exposure photography. They are the impetus behind Moritz's experimentation:

"I LOVE THE SPONTANEITY OF IT ALL, EACH TIME I MOVED THE CAMERA I WOULD GET SOMETHING TOTALLY UNEXPECTED. I THOUGHT, 'WHAT ELSE CAN I DO WITH THIS?"

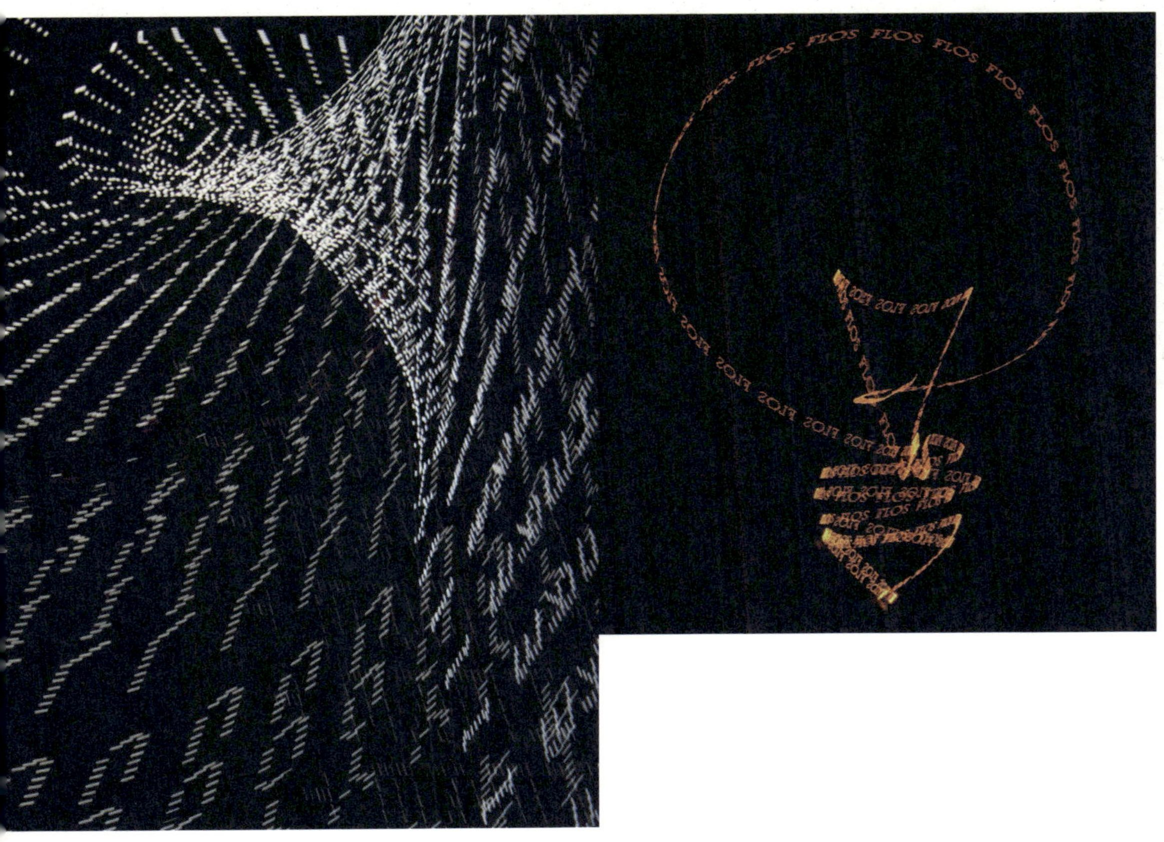

Moritz began to play more actively with persistence of vision, creating images or text in mid air. First, he tried out the simplest form of the idea for an ICA charity auction, making a single LED attachment to a bicycle spoke, programmed to flash on and off as the wheel turns, drawing a smiley face. The next project was a brooch for Flos that, when swept through the air, would spell out the brand name in flashes of red LEDs. Using the technology in a piece of jewellery prefigures Moritz's later step into the realm of clothing and performance props that we see in the martial artist and musician collaborations.

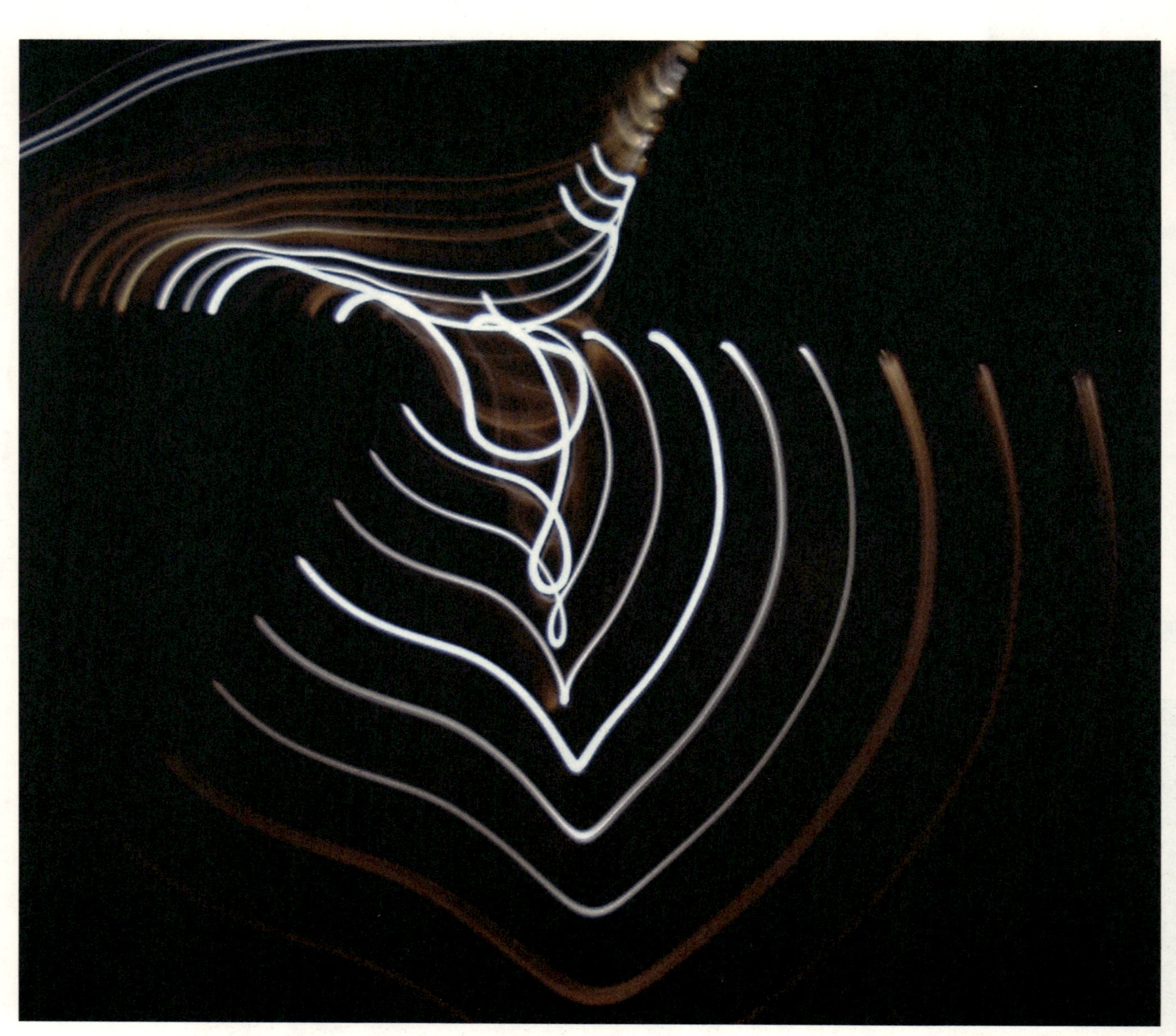

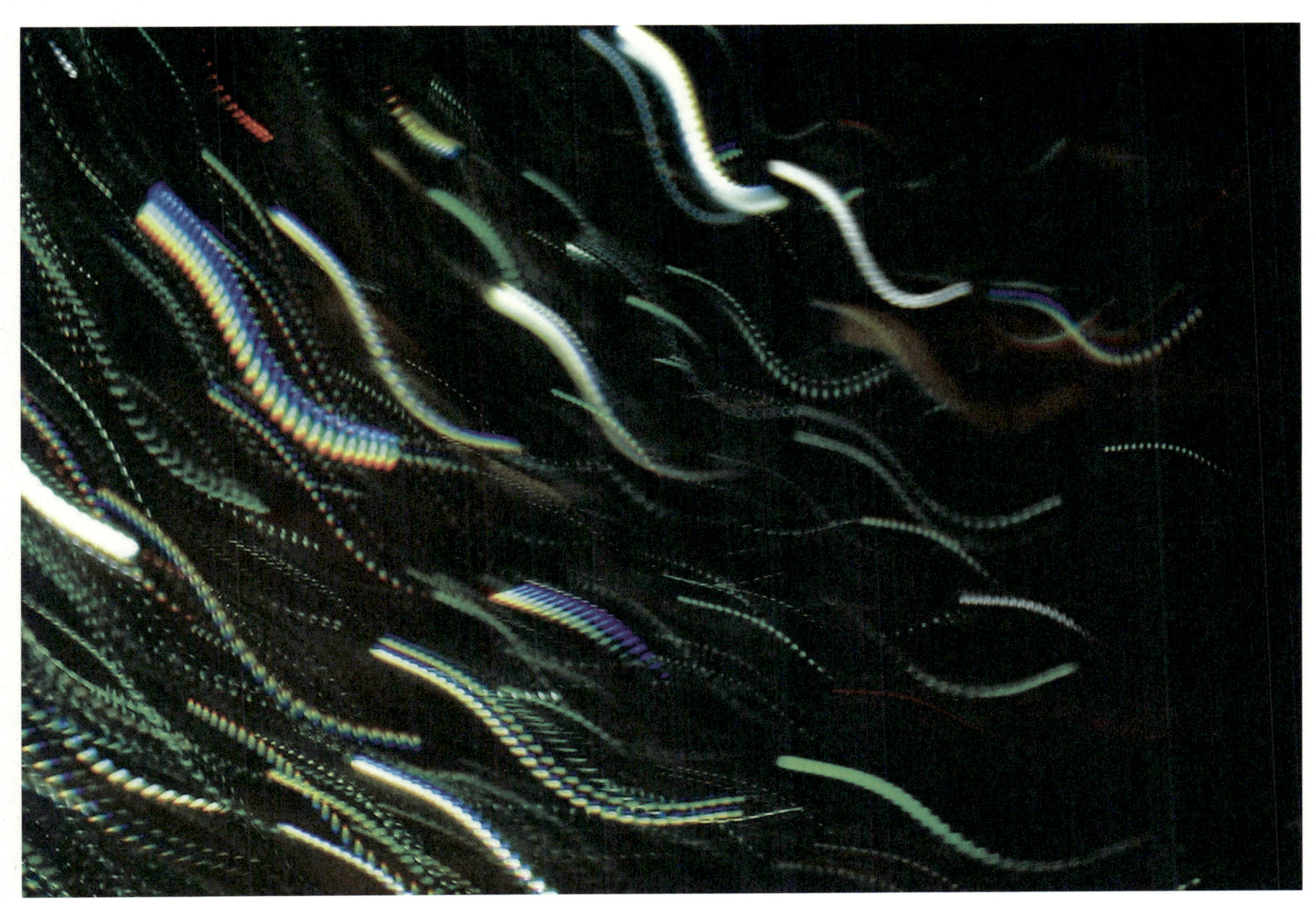

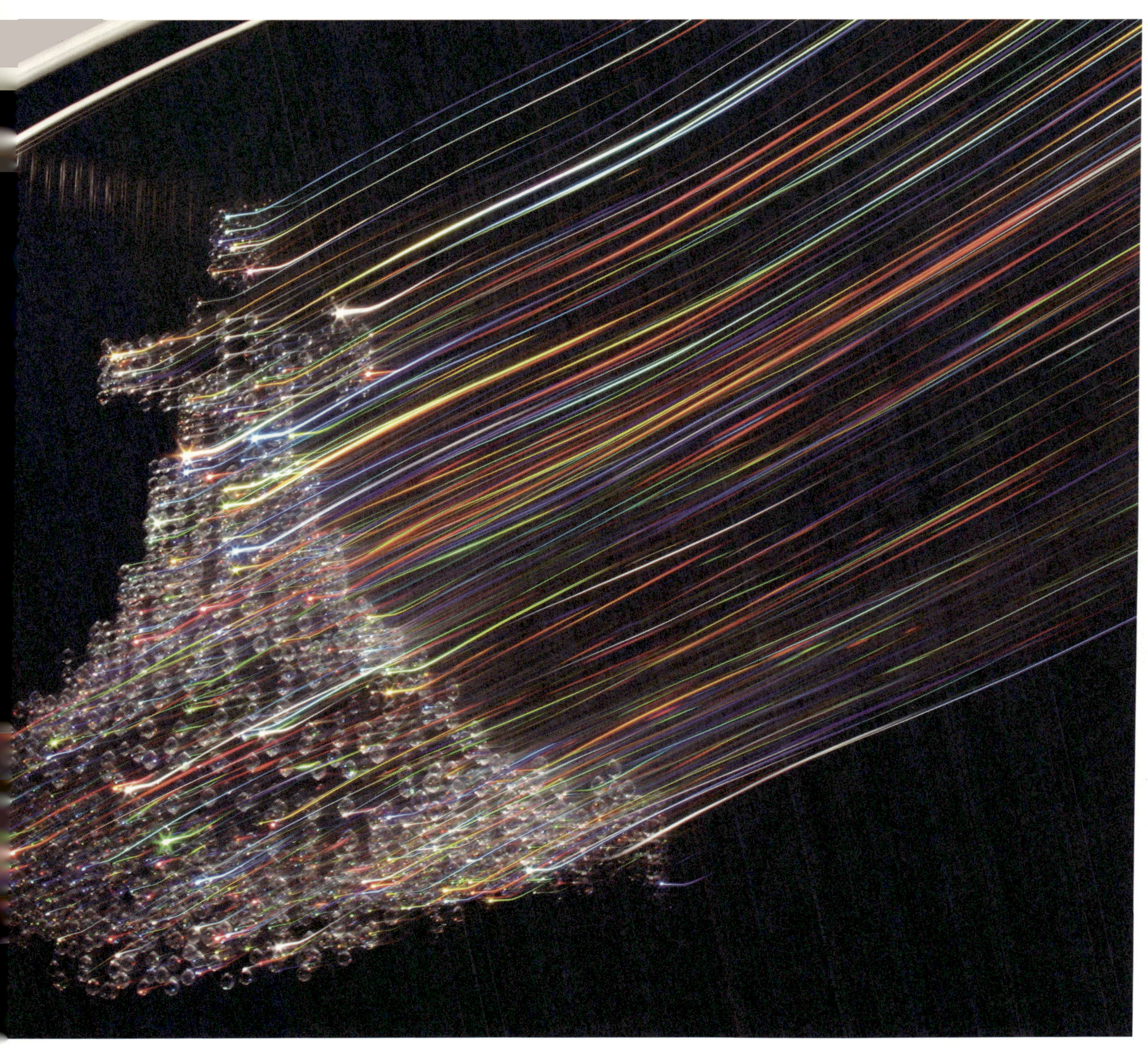

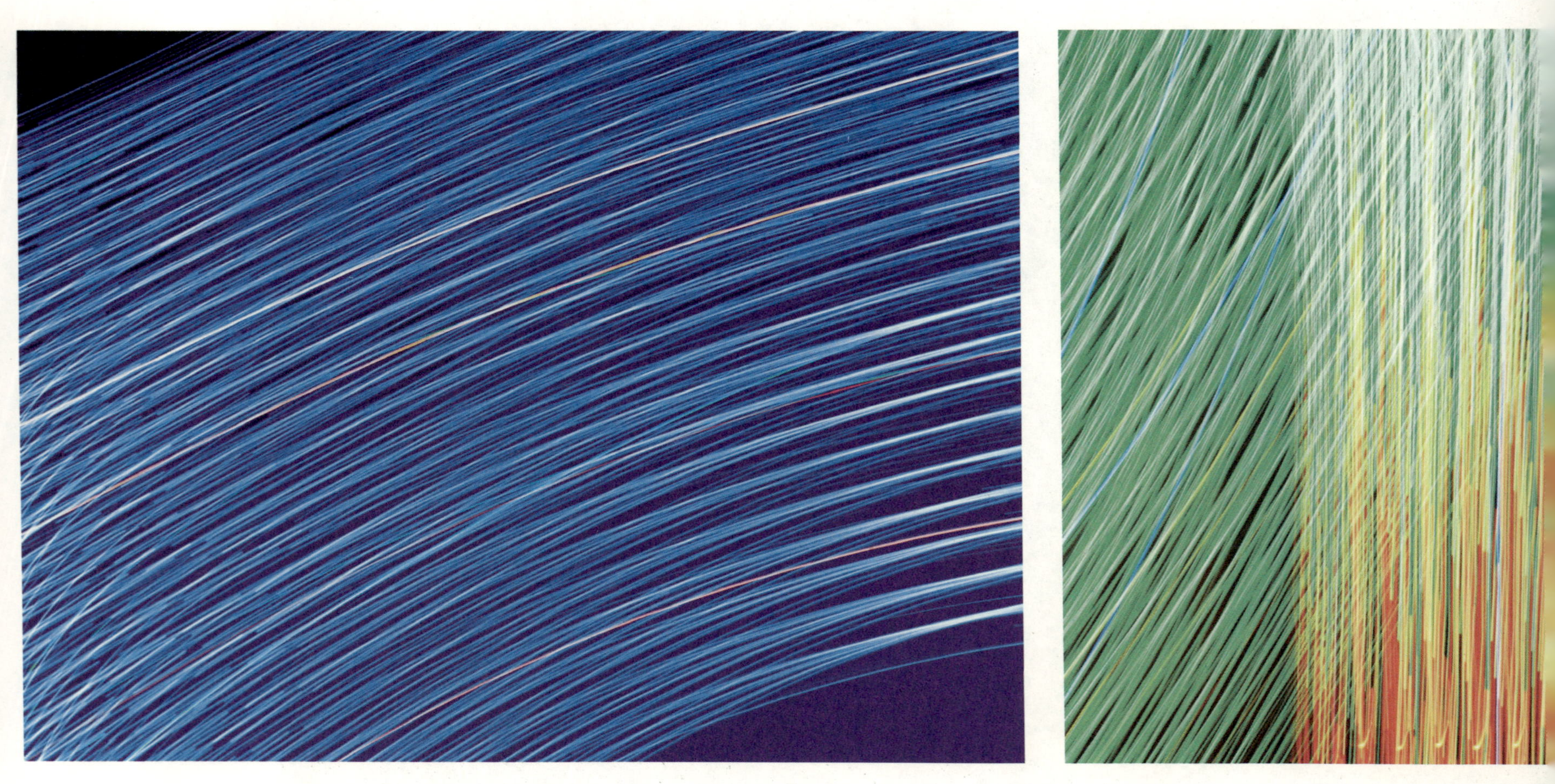

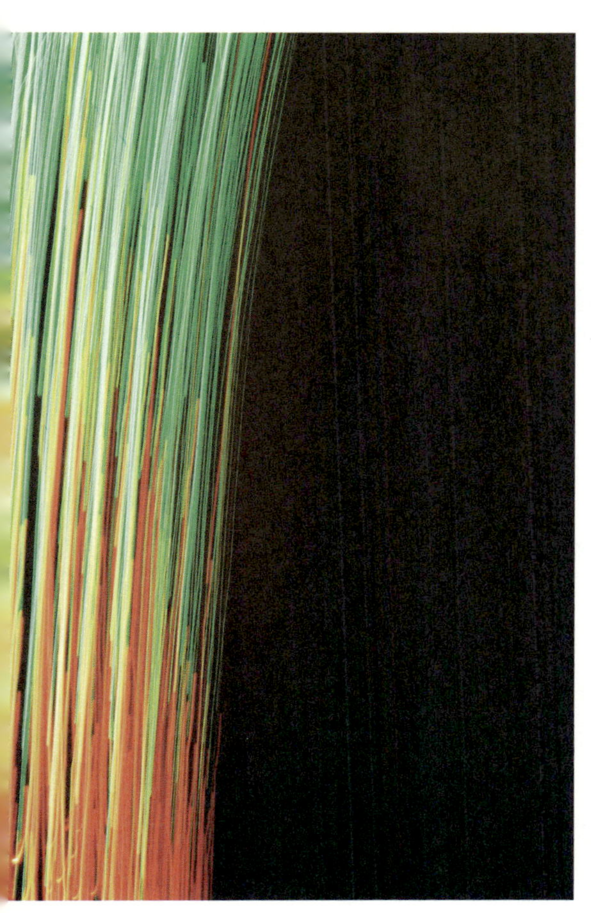

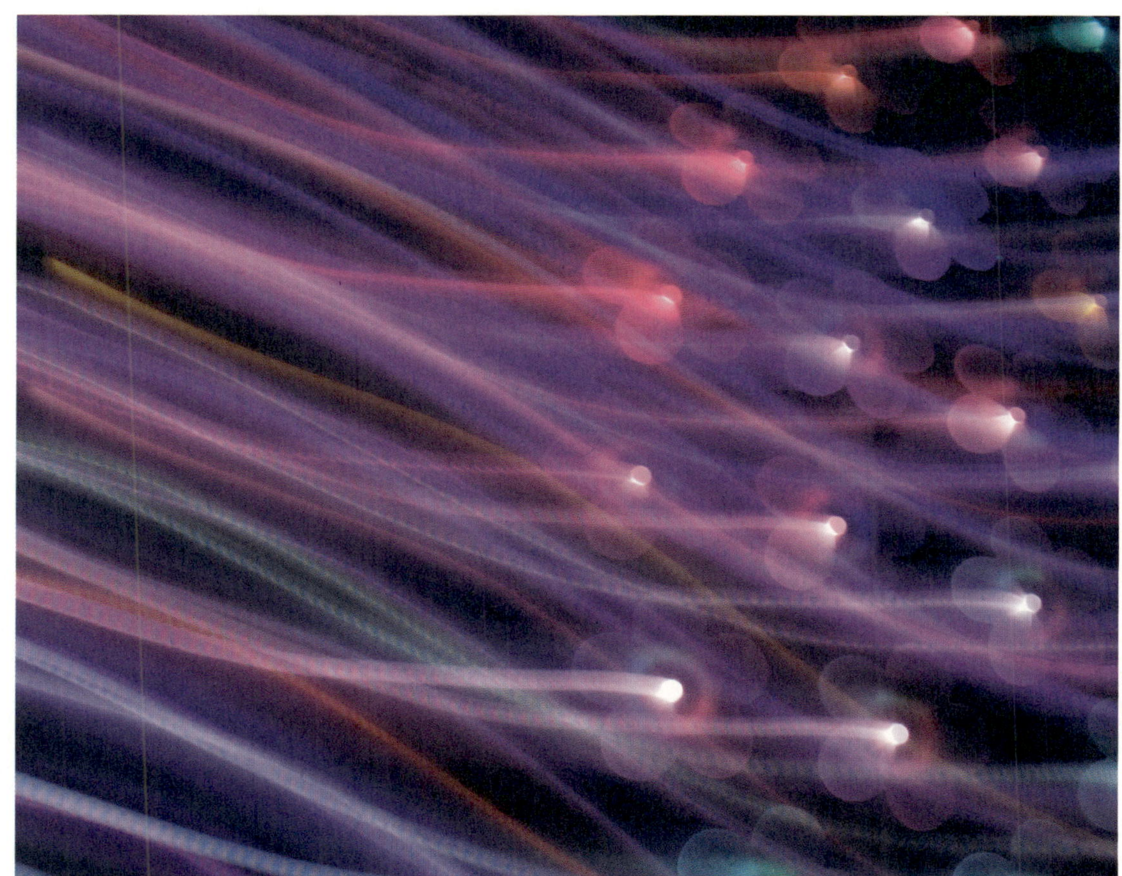

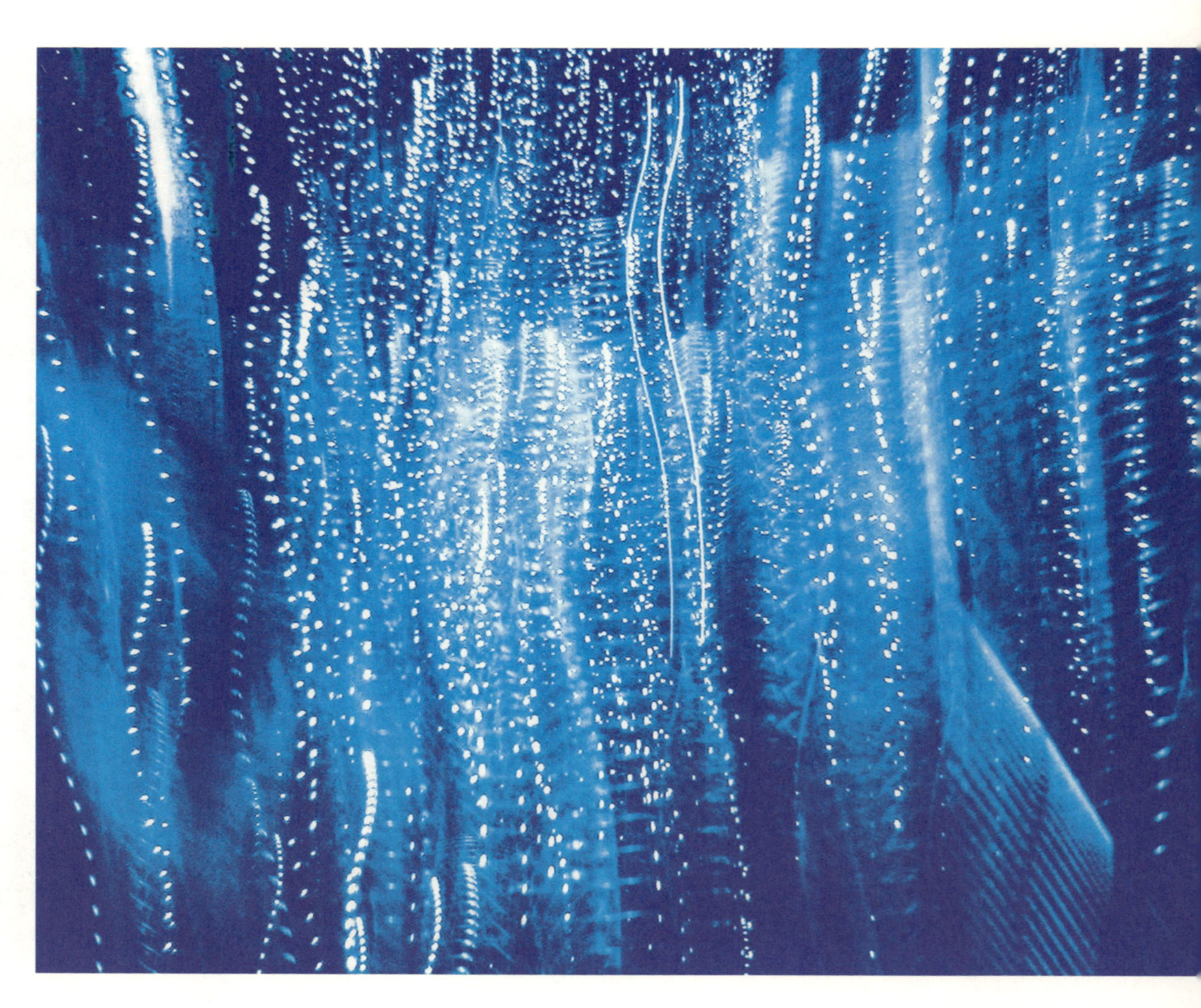

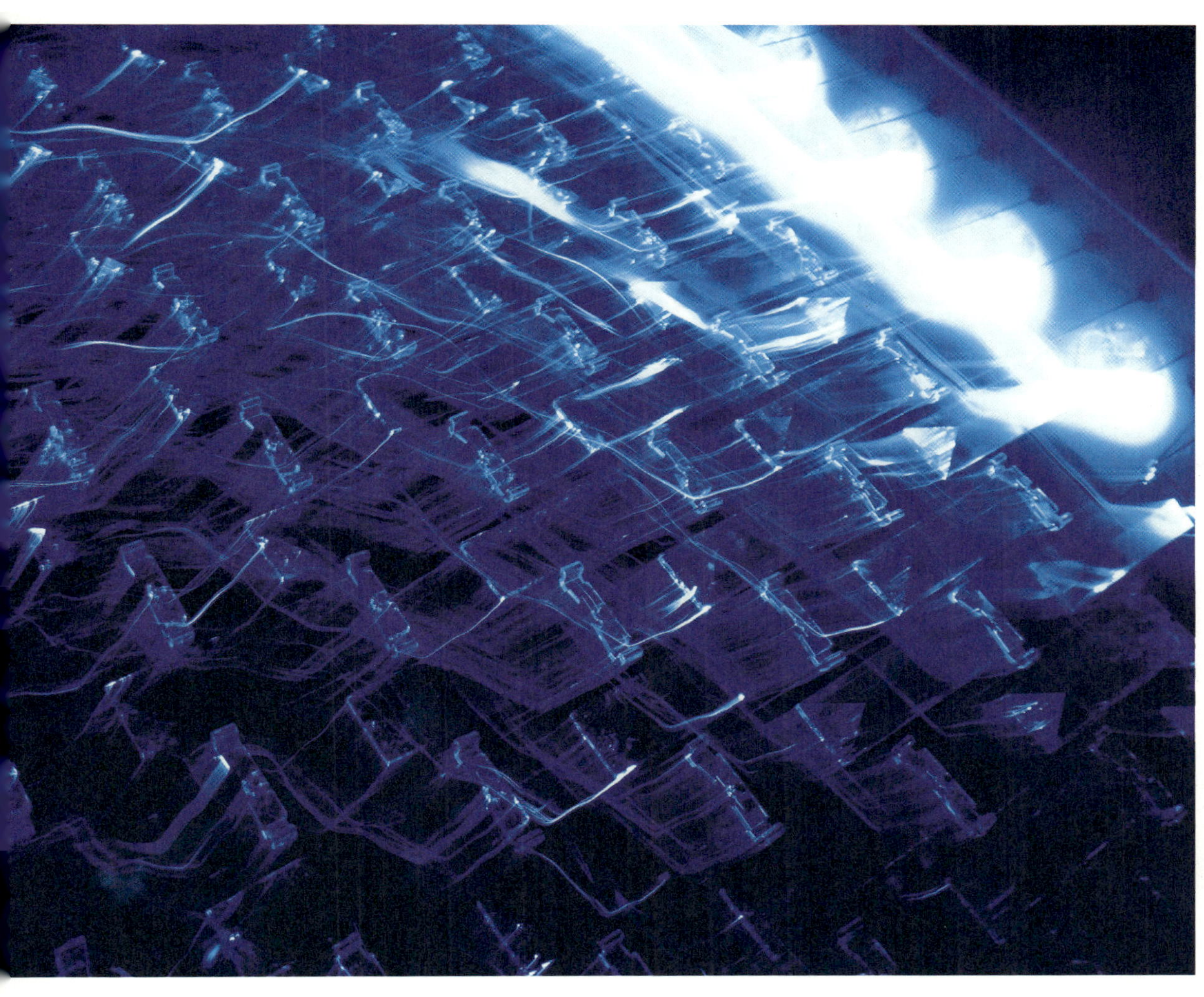

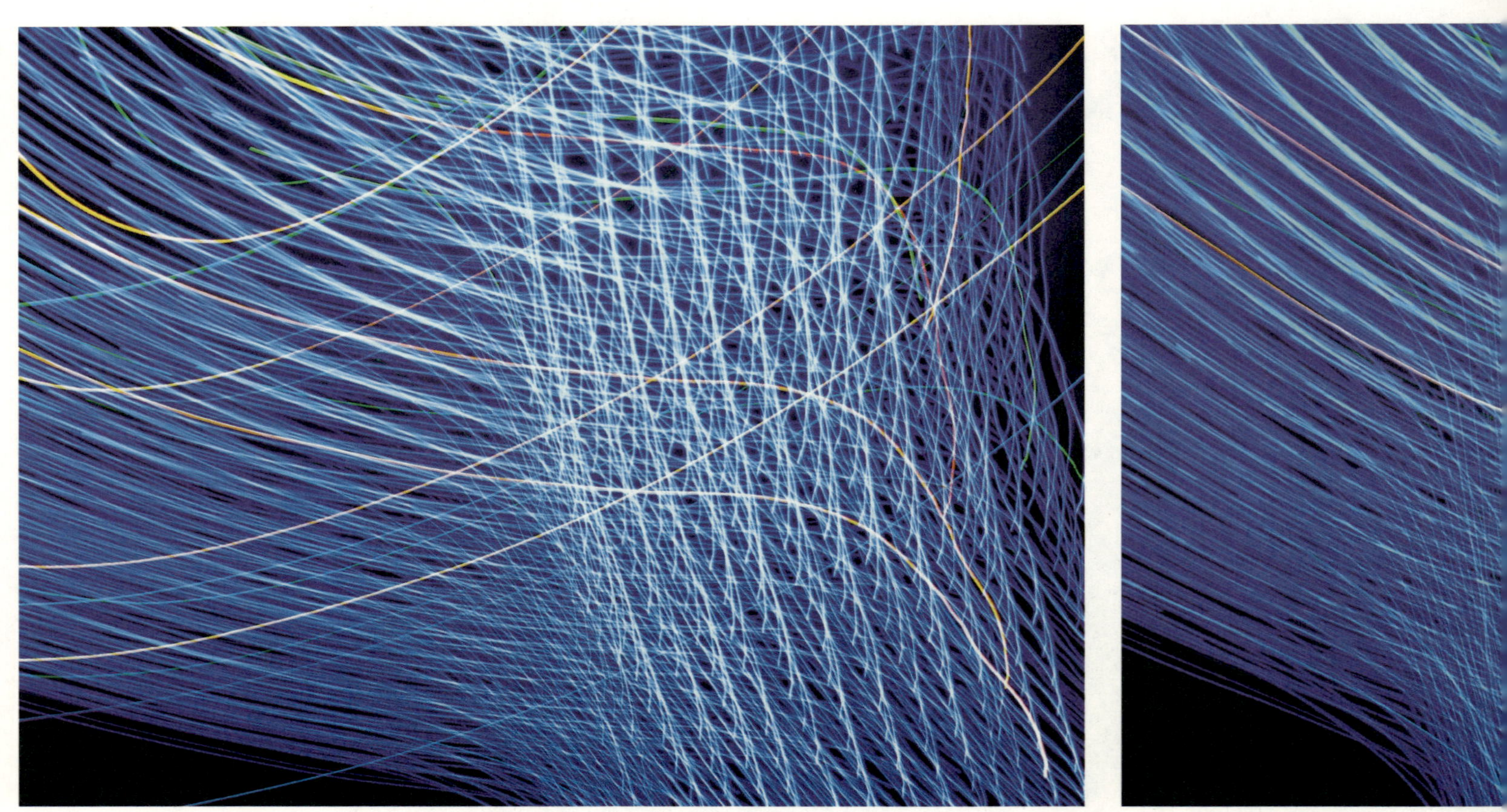

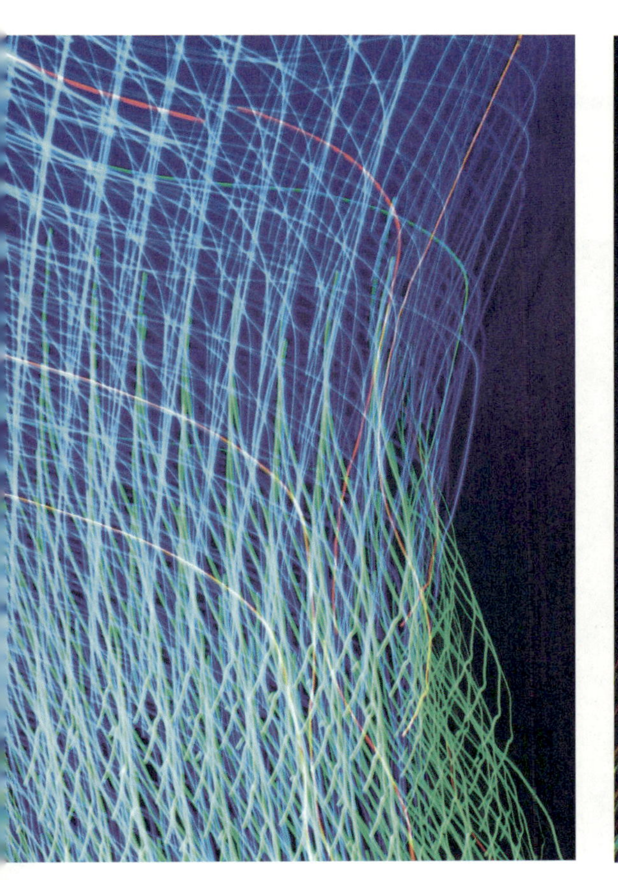

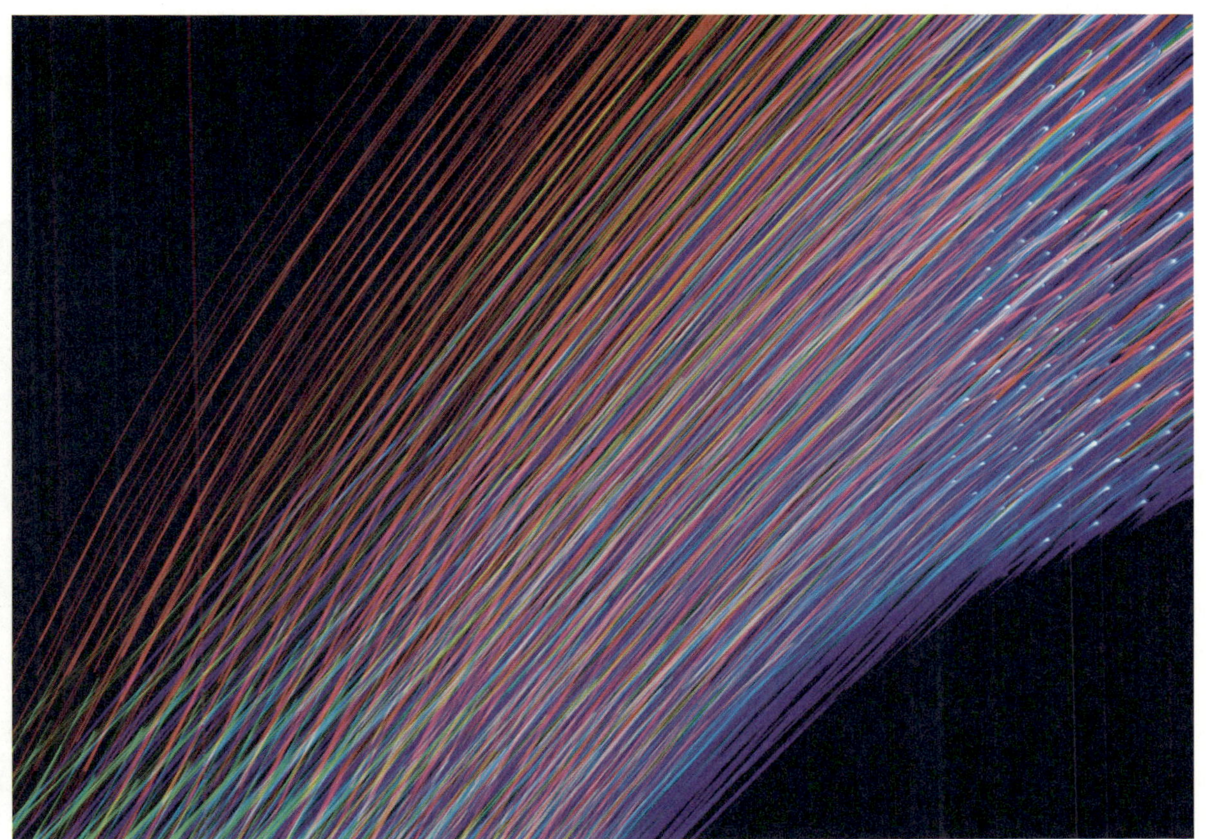

LIGHTEN

These photographs are the result of two workshops run by Moritz alongside the photographer James Harris. The idyllic location is Boisbuchet, a sixteenth-century country estate in the South of France that works with the Pompidou Centre and Vitra Design museum to bring acclaimed artists and designers into their creative community. The two workshops explore movement and light by creating LED-embedded objects to be used after dark in long-exposure photographic compositions.

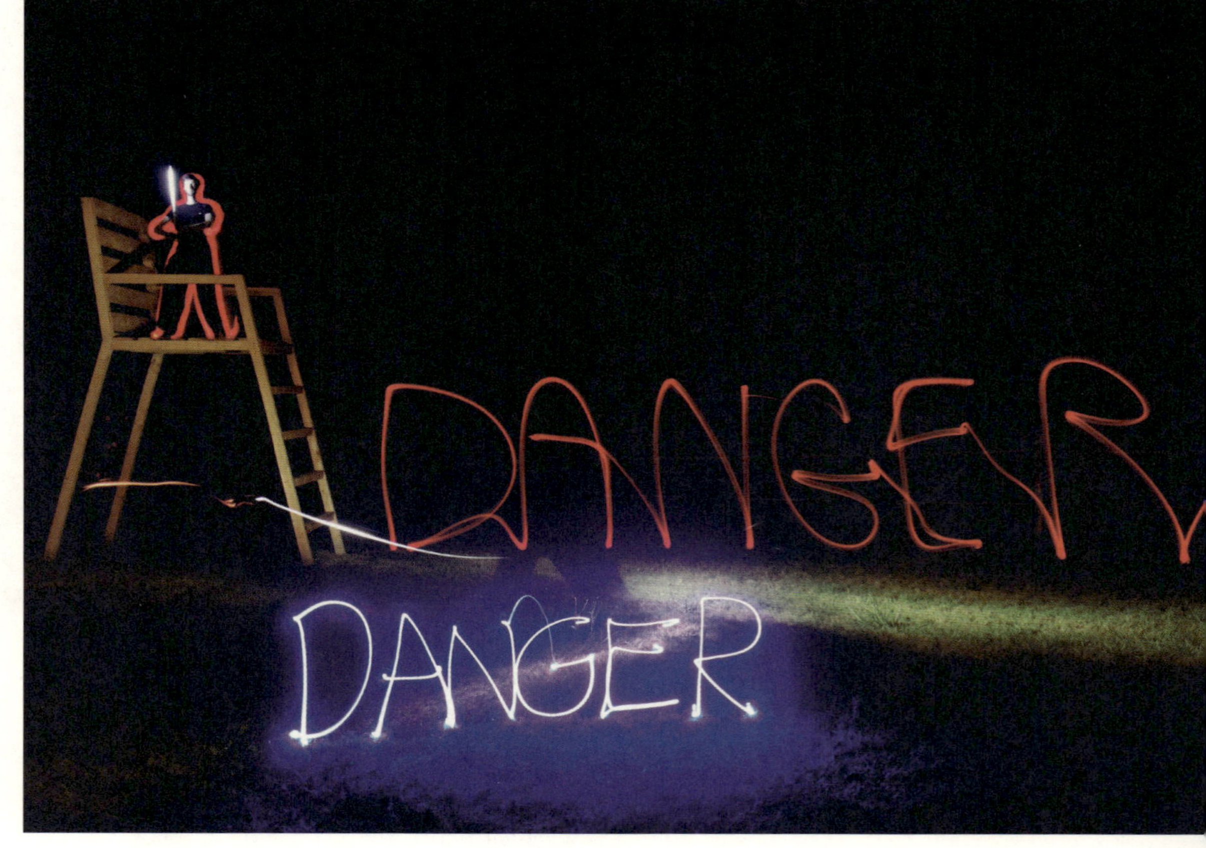

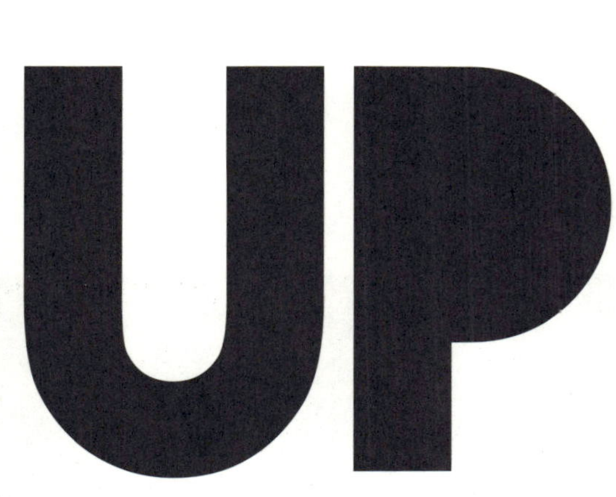

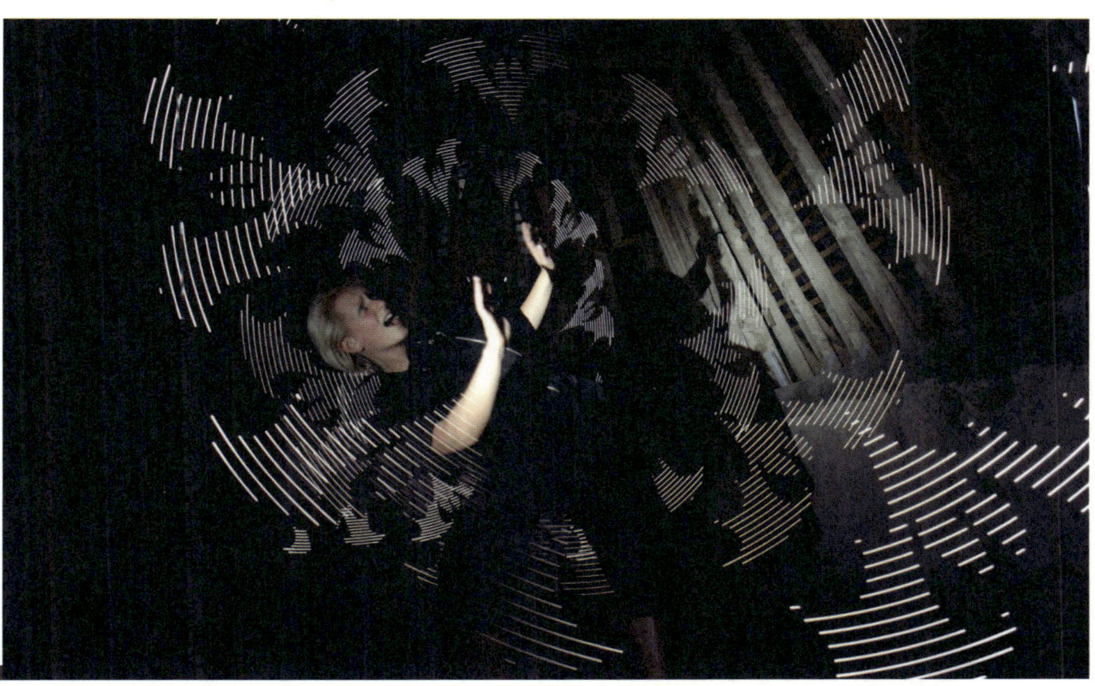

"THE OPPORTUNITY TO EXPERIMENT WITH JAMES HARRIS IN SUCH A MAGICAL LOCATION, STREWN WITH PAVILIONS DESIGNED BY THE LIKES OF SIMON VELEZ AND SHIGERU BAN, WAS A DREAM. WE EXPERIMENTED WITH THIS INCREDIBLE BACKDROP, MAKING OUR OWN PAVILIONS OF LIGHT OR SIMPLY INTERACTING WITH WHAT WAS ALREADY THERE."

The aim of the workshop was not to design a perfect finished product but to provide insights into the design processes and associated challenges of using LED technology and long-exposure photography. It was a mix of mechanical craftsmanship and creative thinking. In the experiments you see fantastical creatures and shapes traced from a single LED light source, as well as graphics – snowflakes, a bat, and a coat of arms. Some of these graphics feature later in the book, in the context of the projects they belong to, but the bats themselves were inspired by the attics of Boisbuchet. They are emblematic of the workshop itself since it is only at night that the LEDs come alive. In the final shot we see a circus of shapes and animals created by the students. This chapter demonstrates lighting, scenery, movement, and photography meshing together to surprising effect. It both informs and is informed by the work we see later in this book.

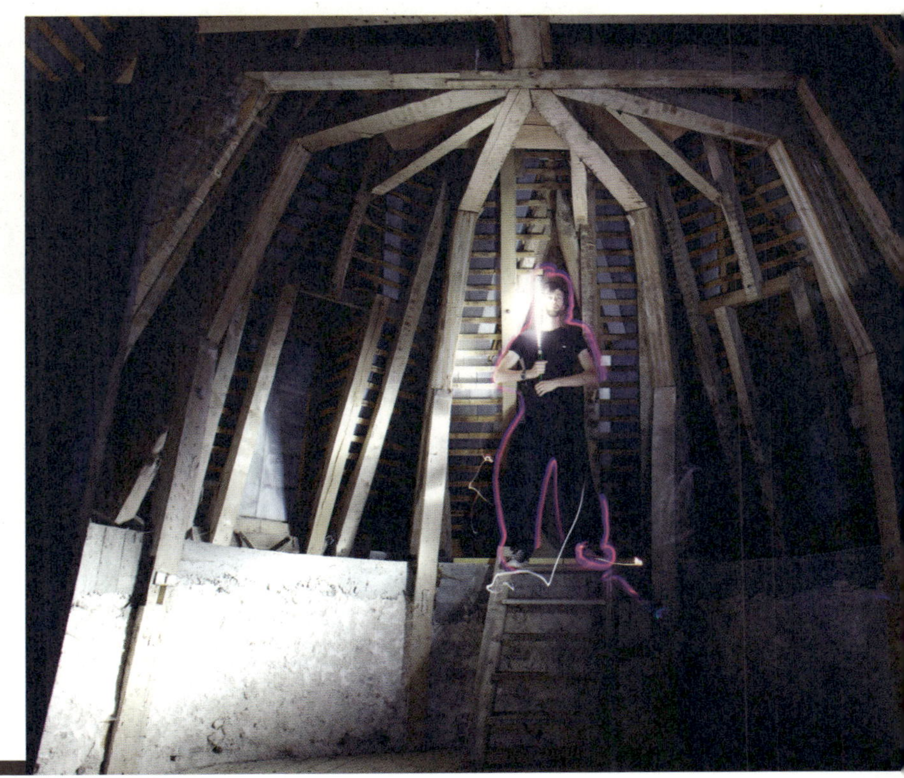

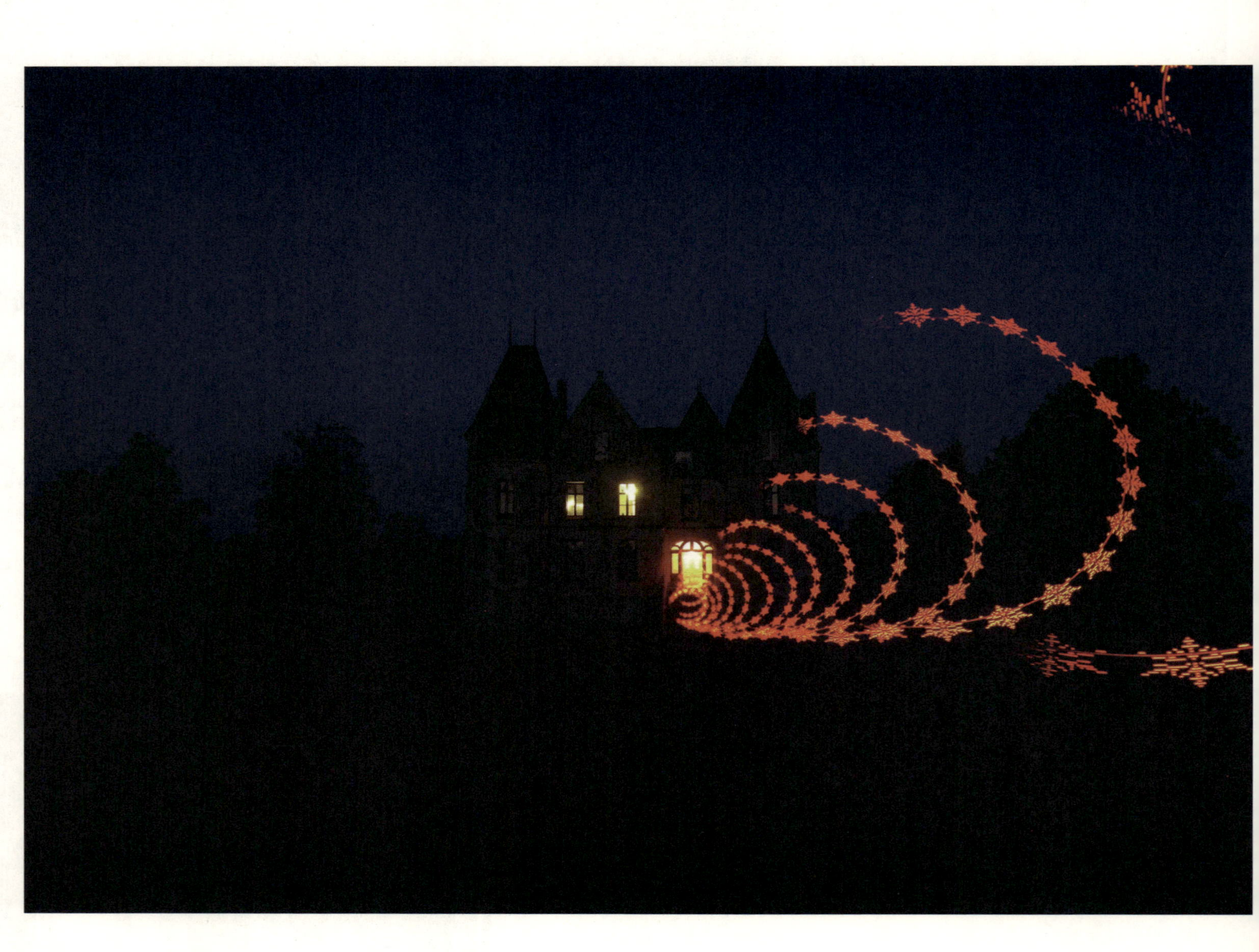

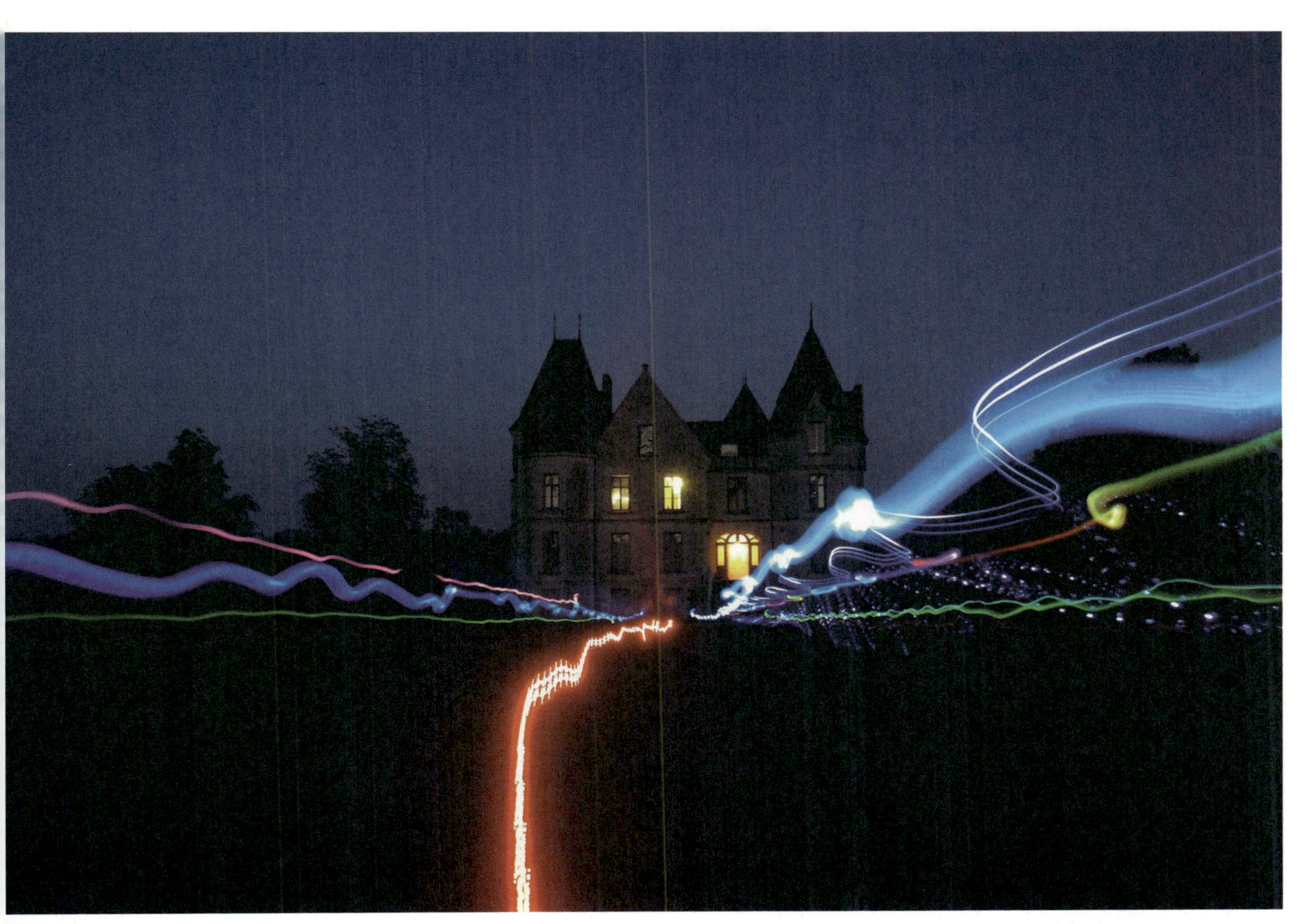

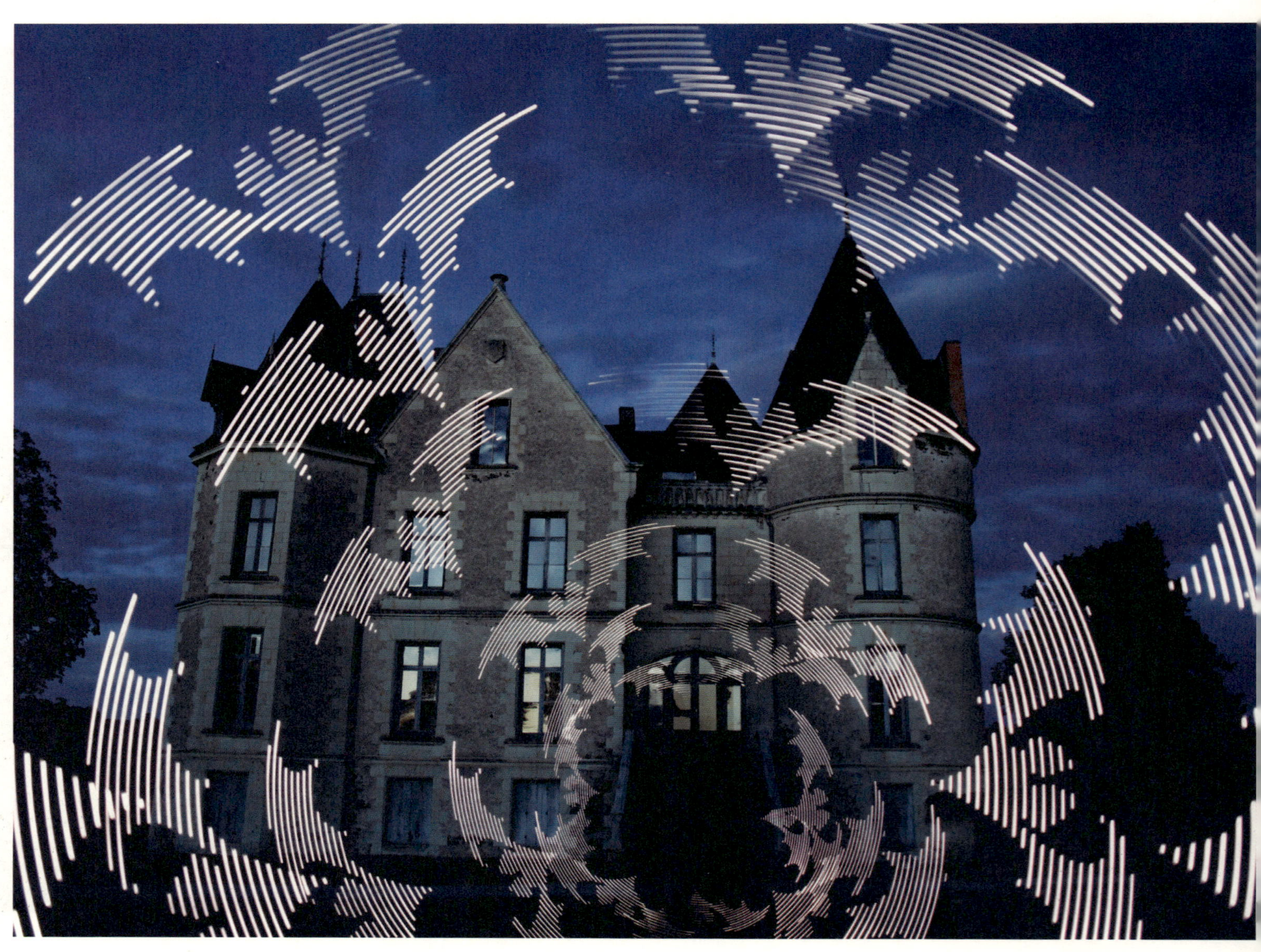

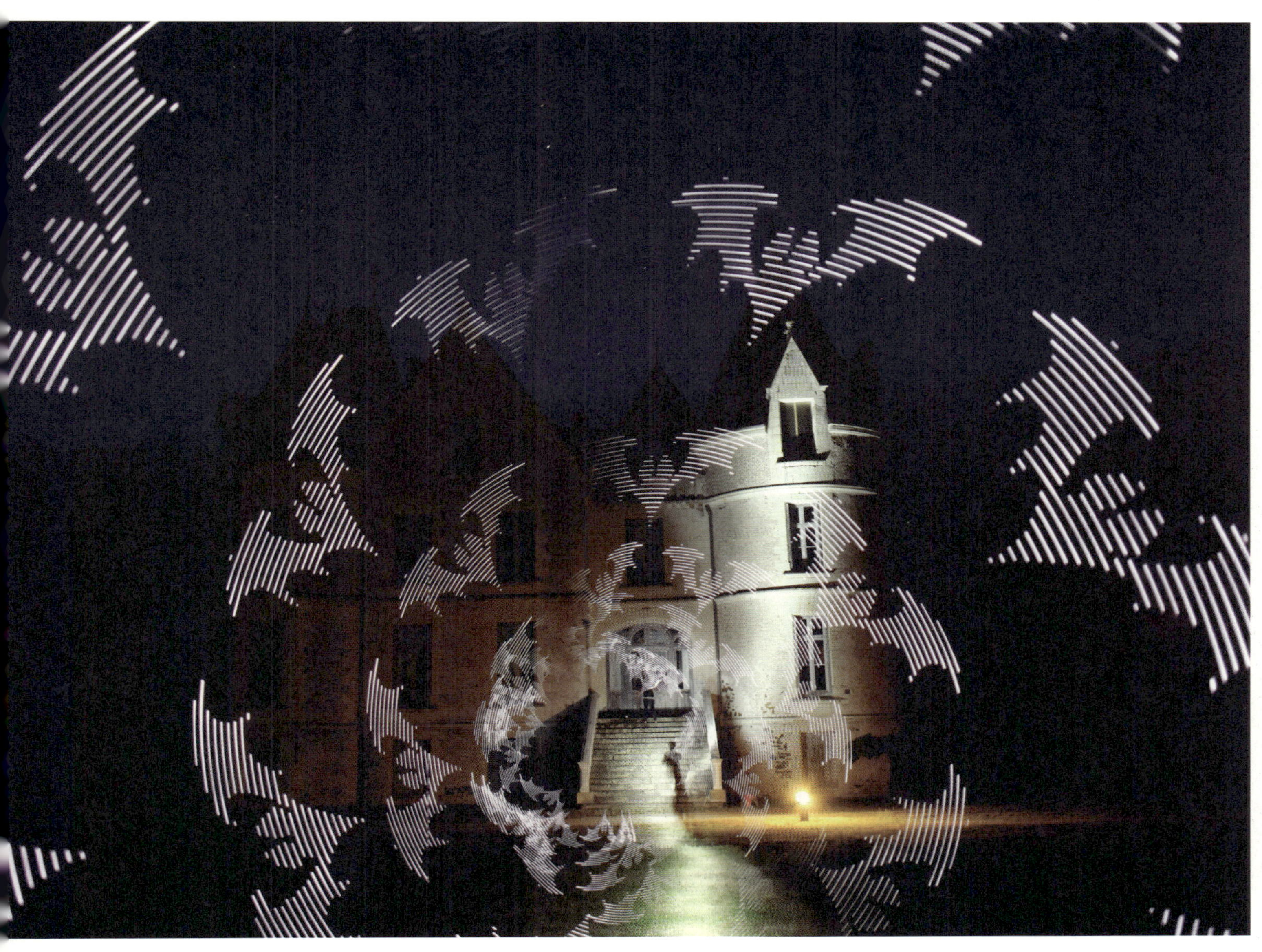

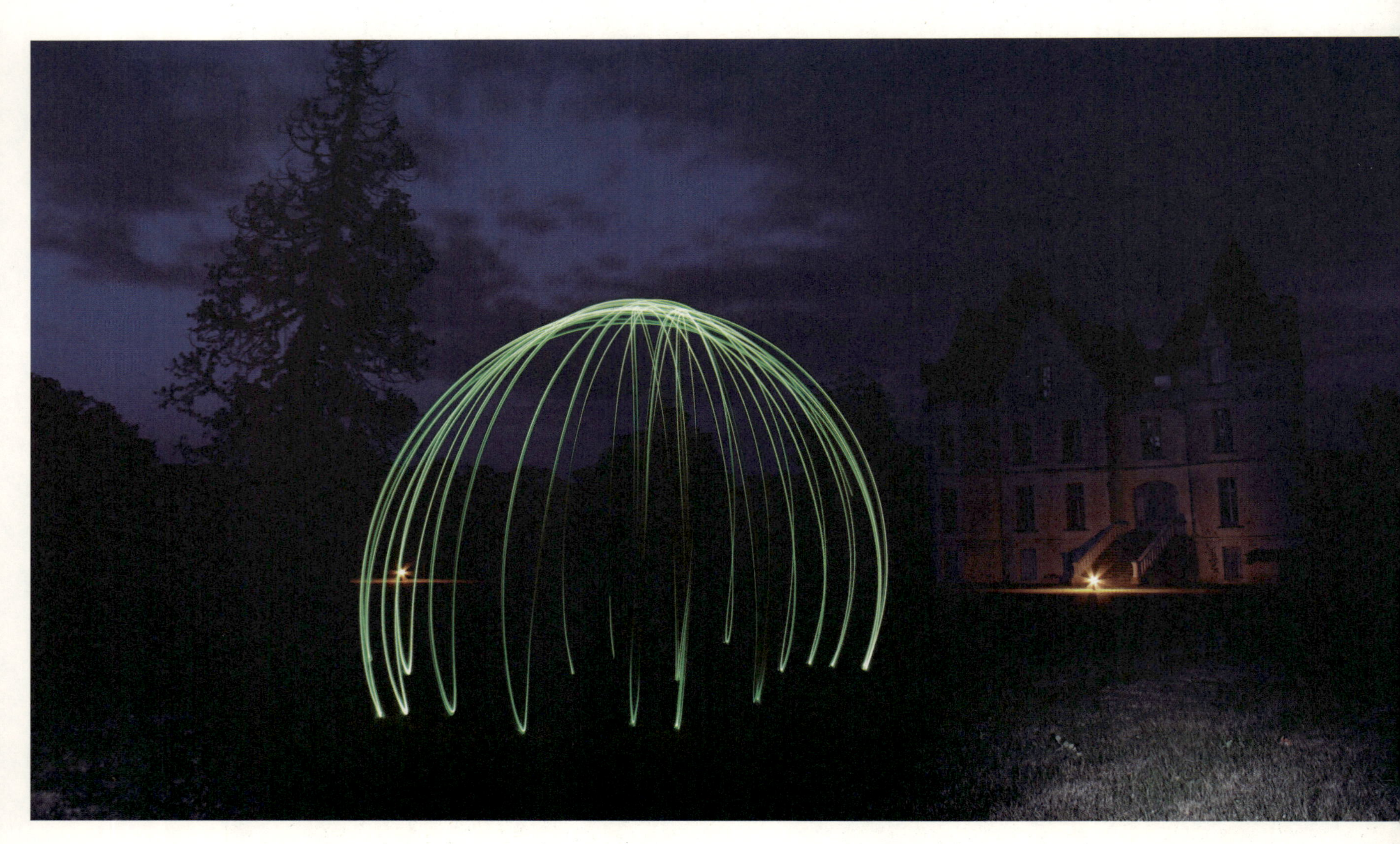

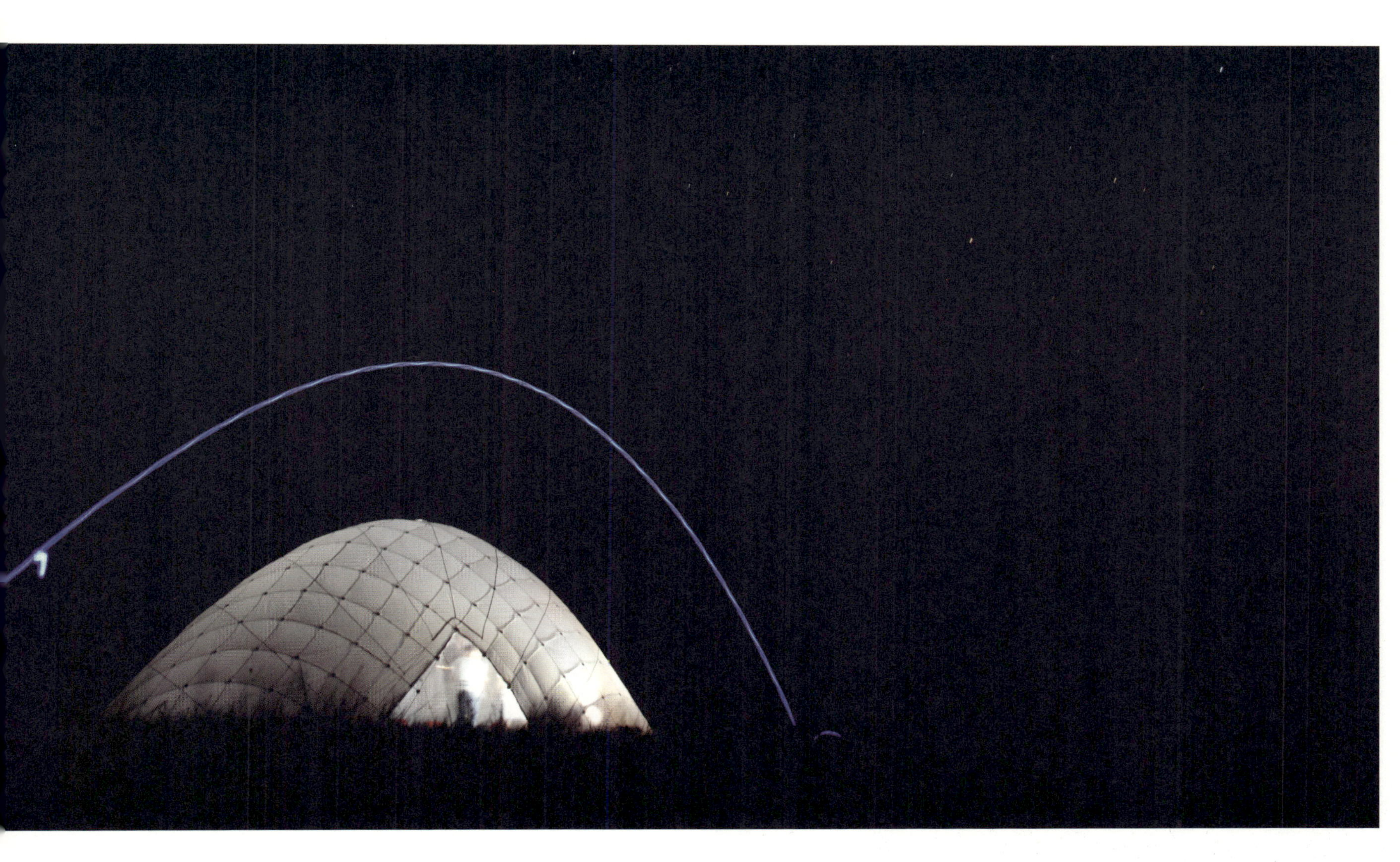

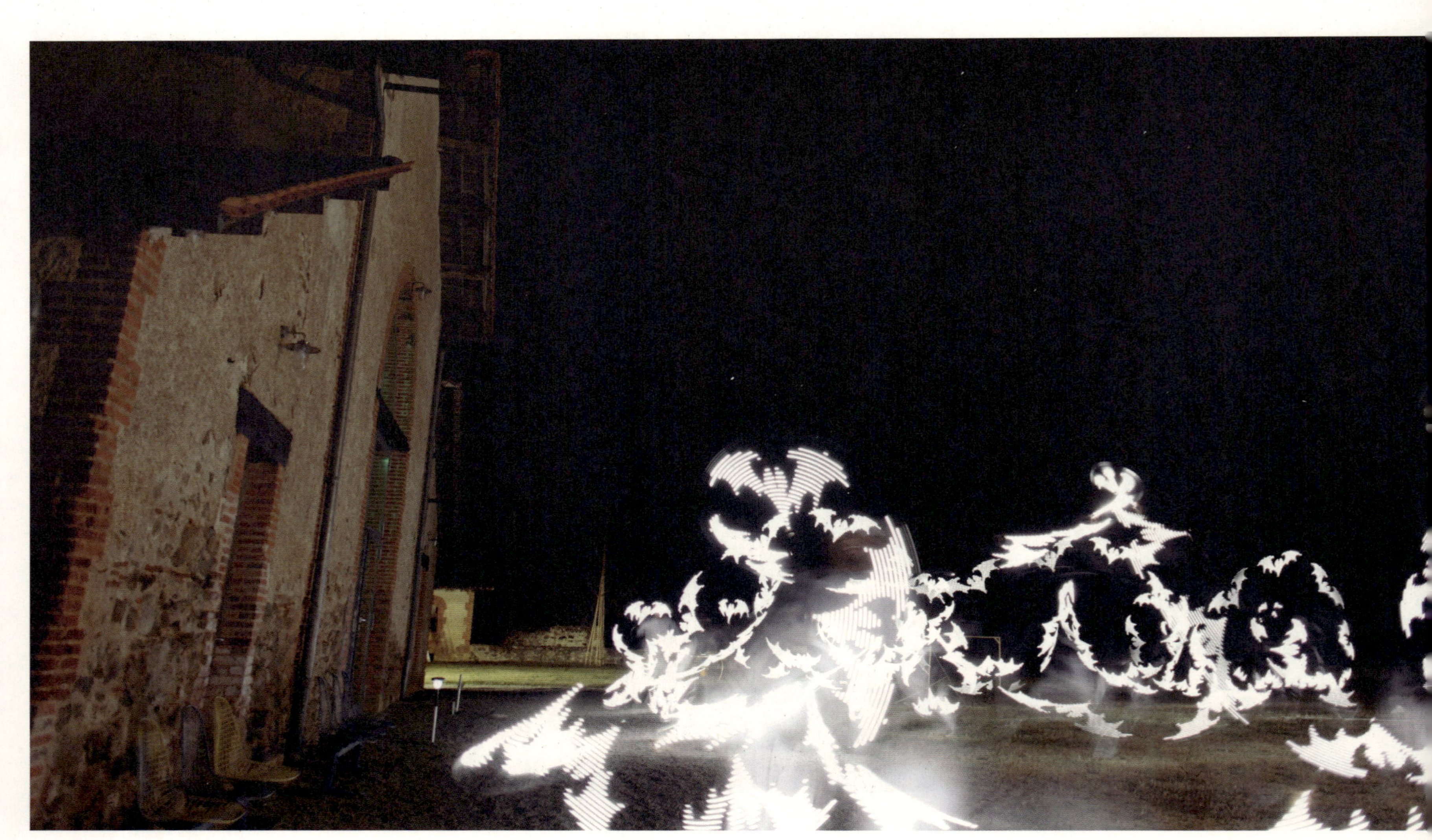

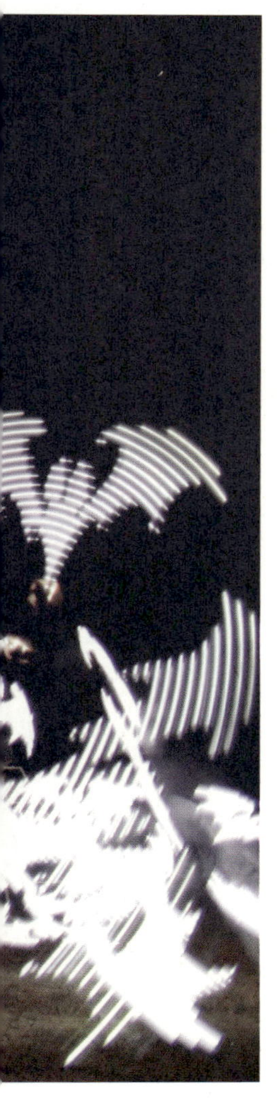

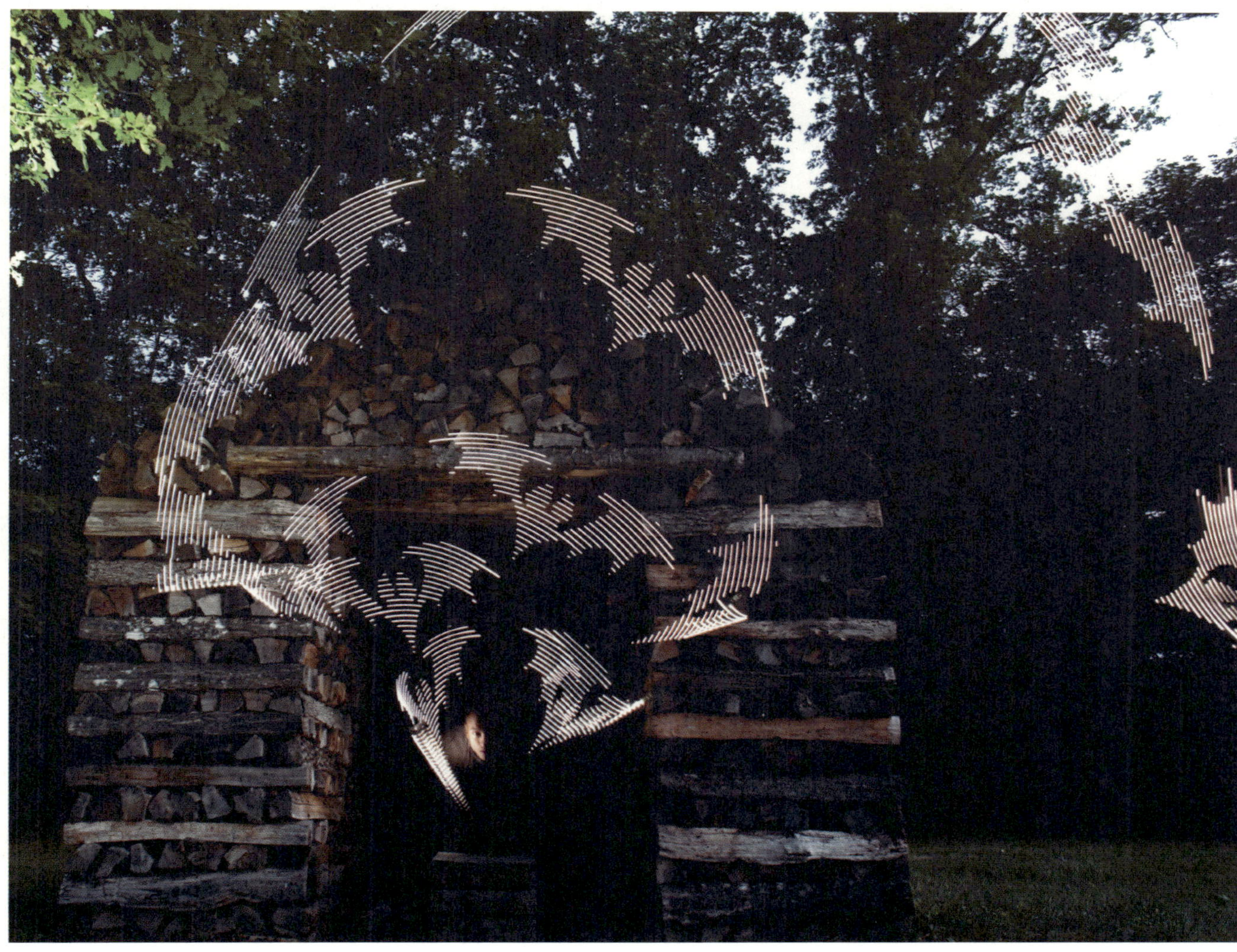

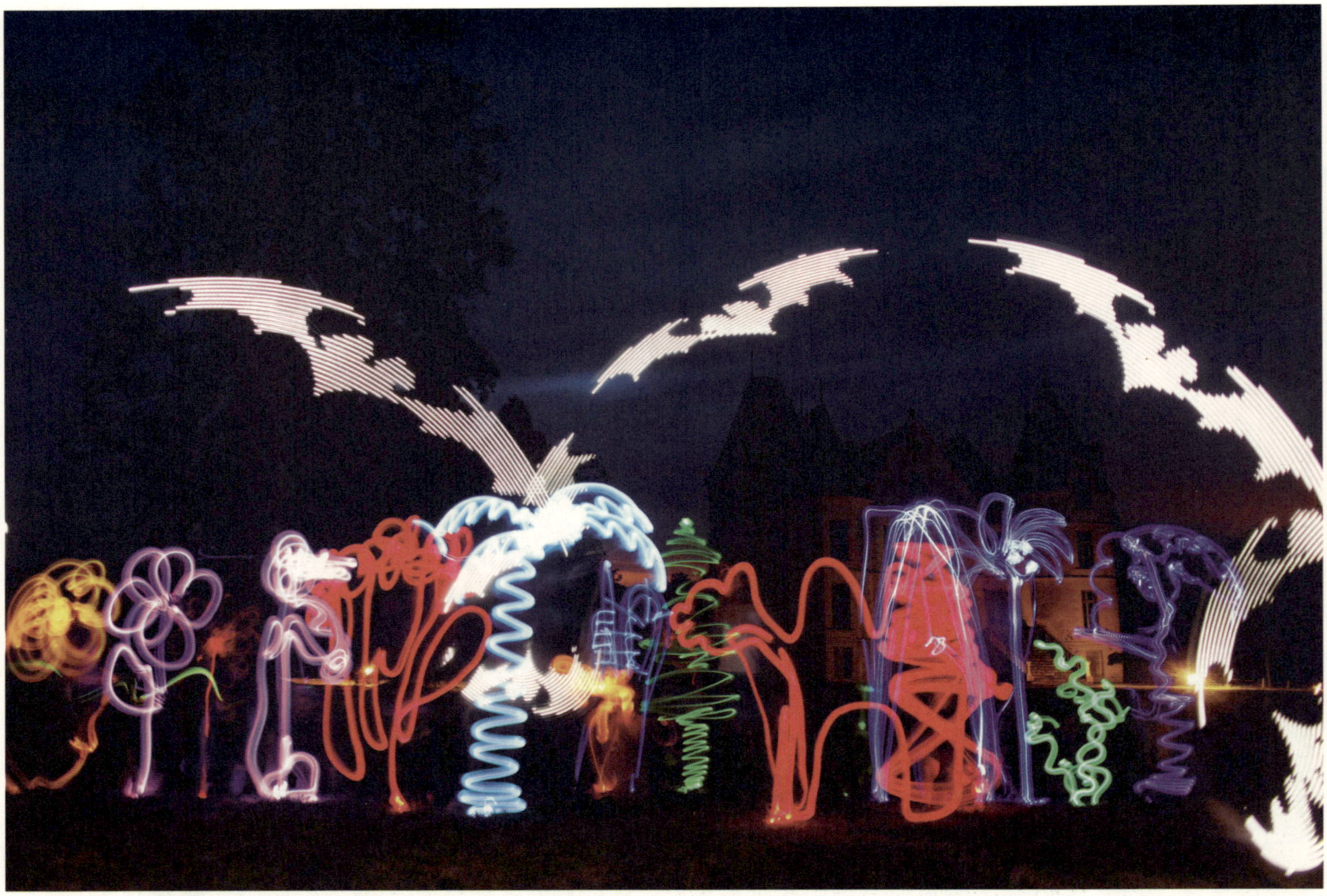

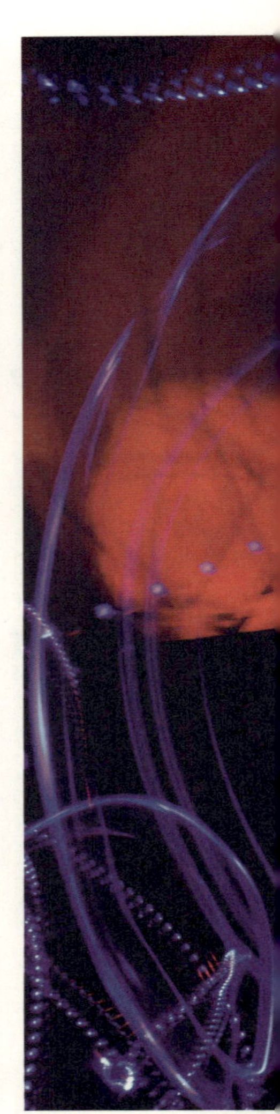

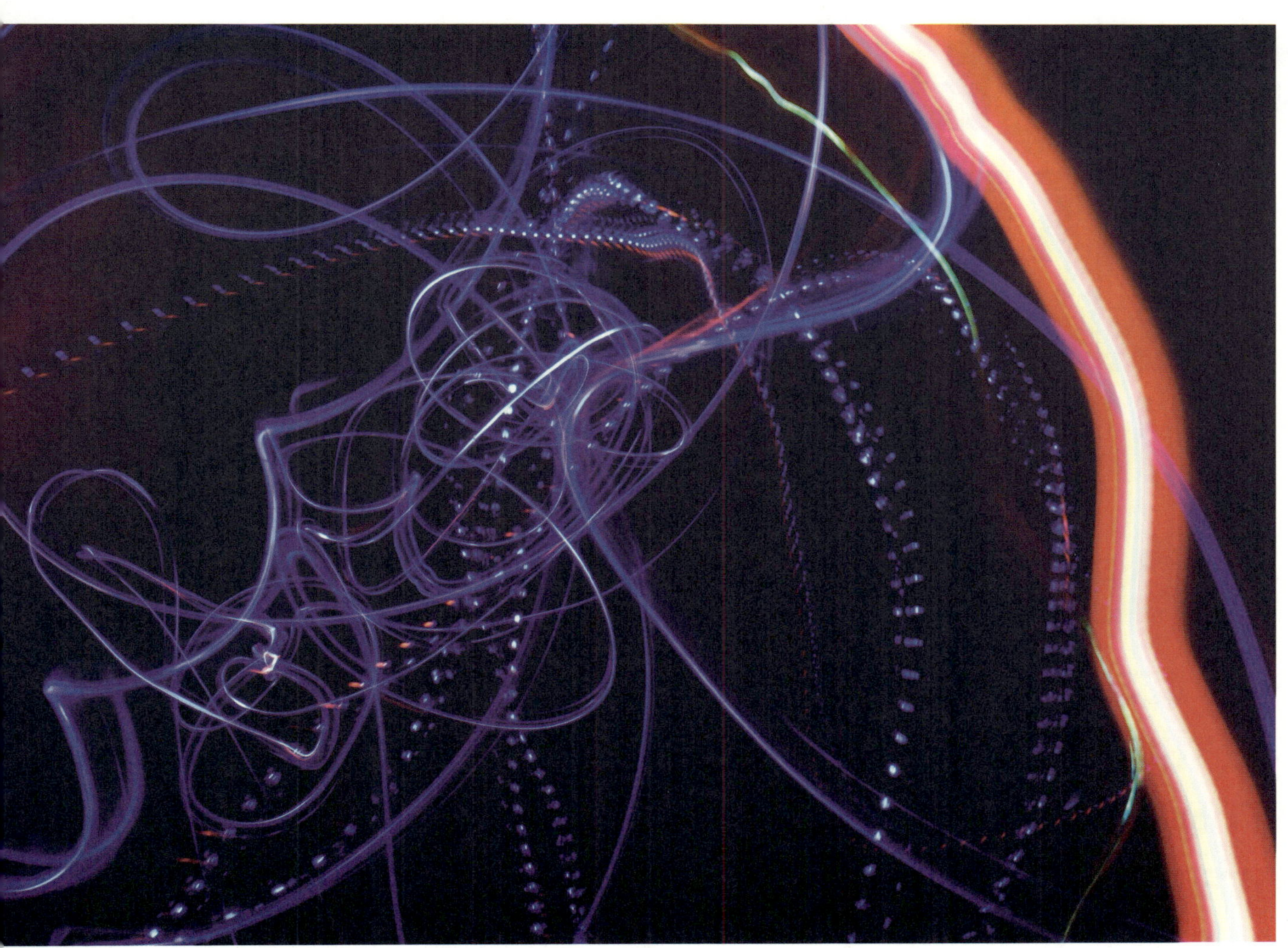

WHEN IN CHINA

In 2010 Moritz was asked to work on the Mercedes-Benz presentation at the Beijing Motor Show. It was the ideal occasion to incorporate wushu, a martial discipline that places emphasis on mentally painting a picture with the sword:

"THE IDEA HAD BEEN IN MY MIND FOR A WHILE, THIS WAS THE PERFECT SETTING, A CAR SHOW FULL OF REFLECTIVE SURFACES AND, MOST IMPORTANTLY, IN BEIJING."

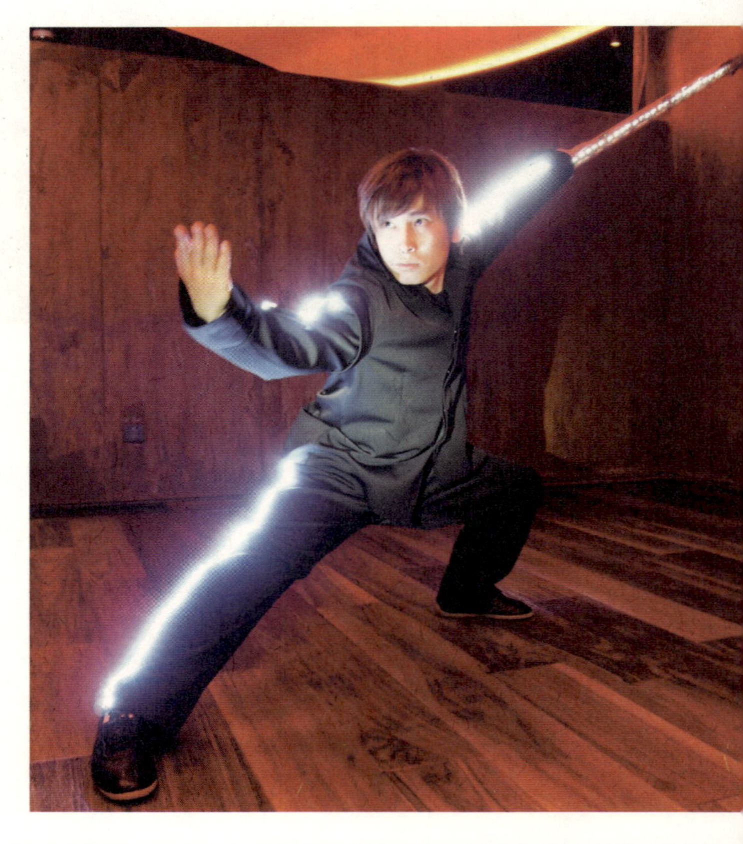

Film and project director Peter Schaul and Mercedes-Benz' global communications agency Oliver Schrott Kommunikation then enrolled some of the UK's most established masters of wushu, karate, acrobatics, dance and stunt acting: Adam Rae, Steven Coleman and Erol Ismail. Through experimenting together they were able to create a dynamic LED-studded weapon, and innovative mixed discipline choreography to complement it. The sword was chosen both for its agility and sweeping movements, ideal for expressing the LED graphics. This choreography was to be taught to fourteen accomplished martial artists based in Beijing before the show.

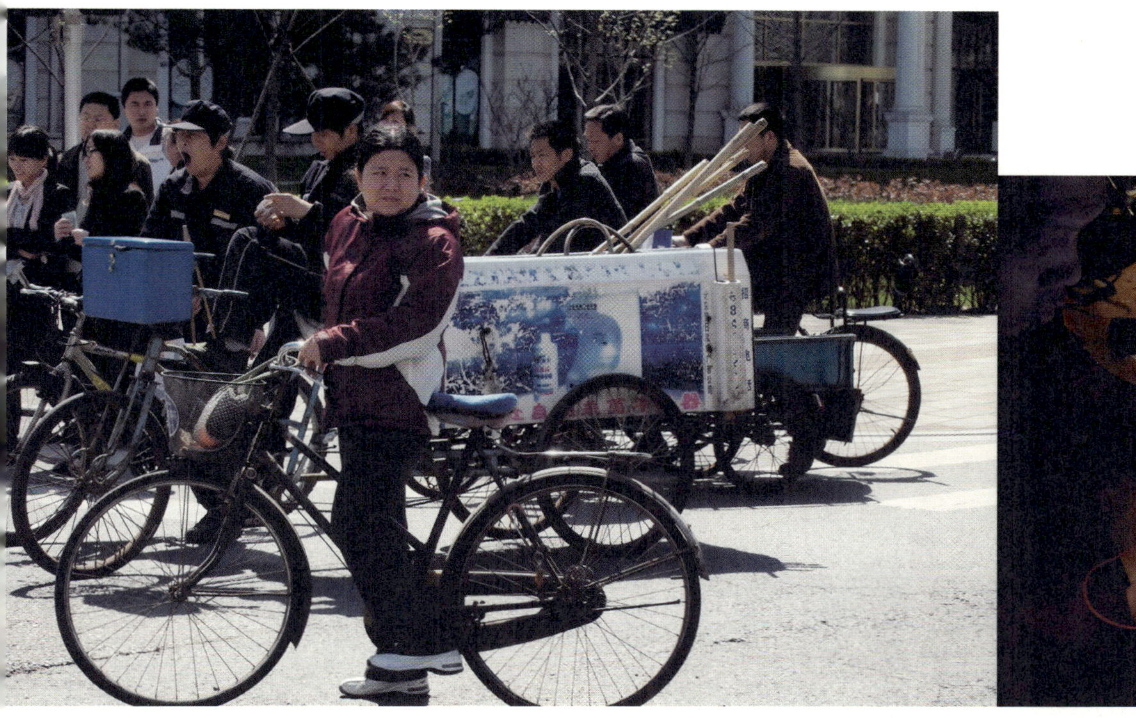

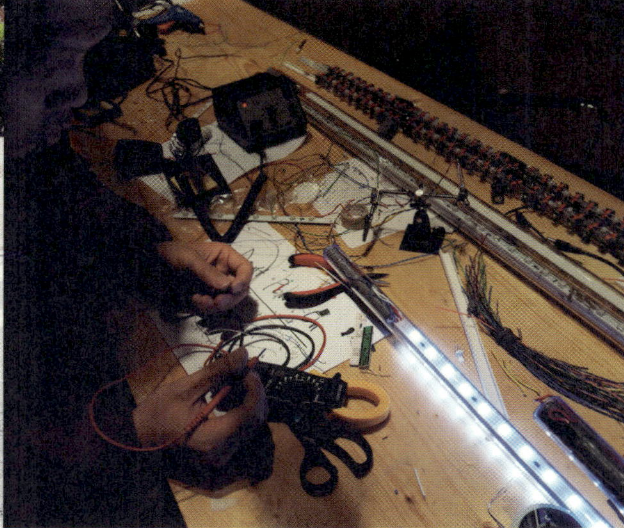

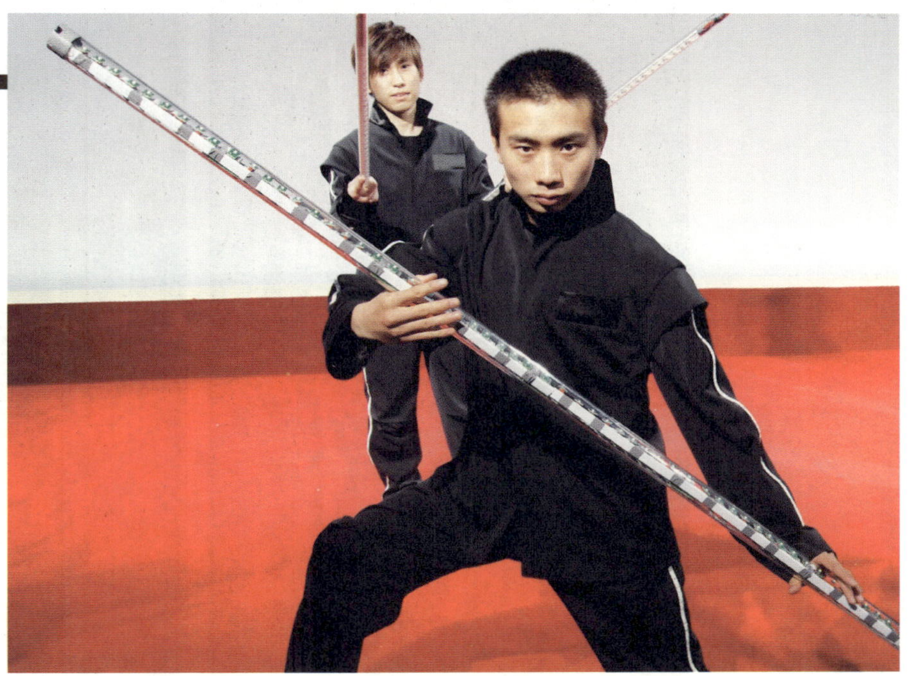

Unfortunately, not everything went to plan. The show was to take place shortly after Milan Design Week where Moritz would be working up until the last minute. Far away the epic Icelandic ash cloud erupted, causing the highest level of air travel disruption since the Second World War. Designers from across the world were stranded in Milan, fellow London-based designers were embarking on 14 hour long train rides back home, while Moritz was wondering how on earth he was going to get to Beijing in just a few days. Thankfully, the Mercedes-Benz team came to the rescue just in time, arranging special transport 5000 miles across the world. Moritz arrived in Beijing to find out that the ubiquitous ash cloud had struck again, leaving all the materials for the show stranded in Belgium. Everything had to be sourced locally and remade from scratch.

The show, miraculously, went off without a hitch. Afterwards, in the red-lit hotel atrium the team began experimenting and, encouraged by the photographic results, tried out new moves. Liberated from the choreography, they focused on who could get the most interesting photographic effects from this new aesthetic weapon:

"THE COMMUNION OF THIS ANCIENT ART WITH MODERN TECHNOLOGY WAS EXACTLY WHAT I HAD IMAGINED IT TO BE. IT WAS GREAT TO SEE THE MOVES OF THE SWORD VISUALISED, SLICING THROUGH THE AIR. LIKE A JAZZ MUSIC JAMMING SESSION, THE RESULTS WERE SPONTANEOUS BUT EXPRESSED THROUGH THE PRECISE TECHNOLOGY IN THE SWORD."

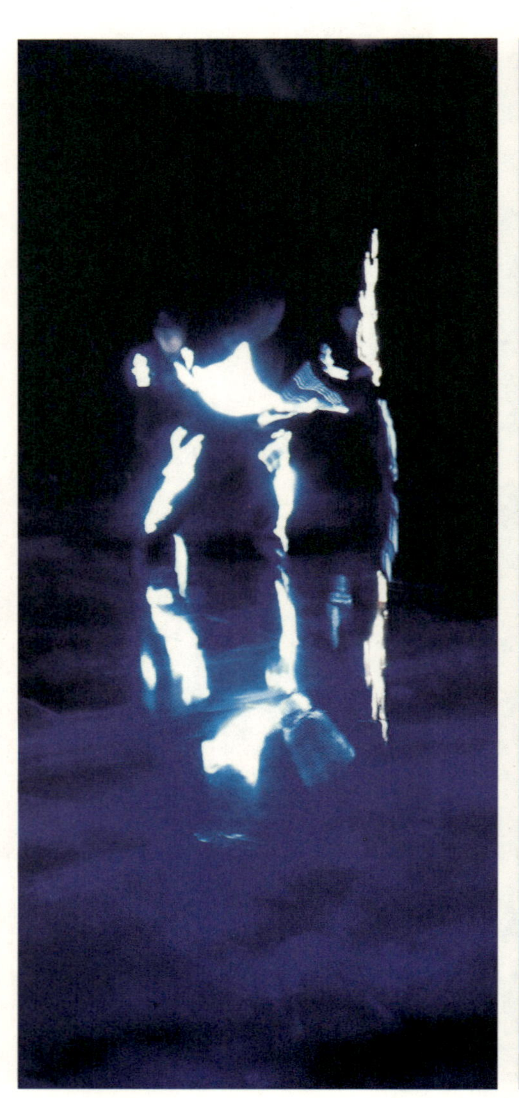
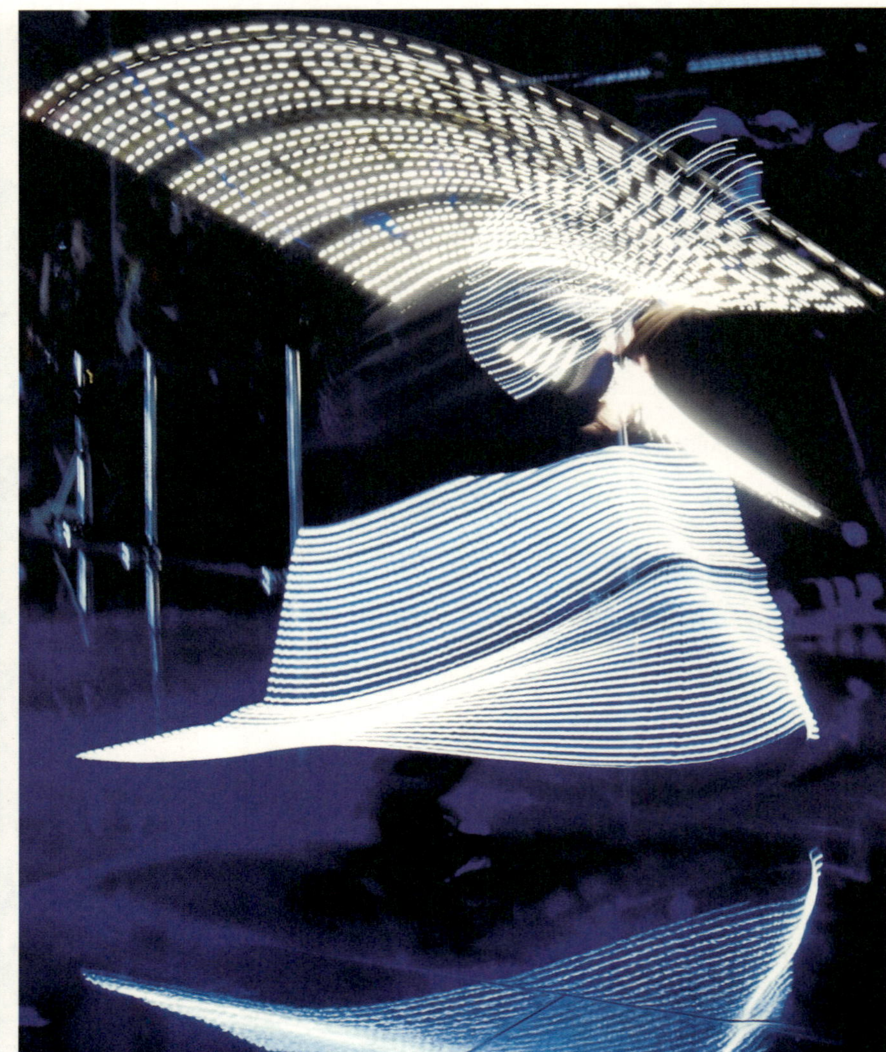

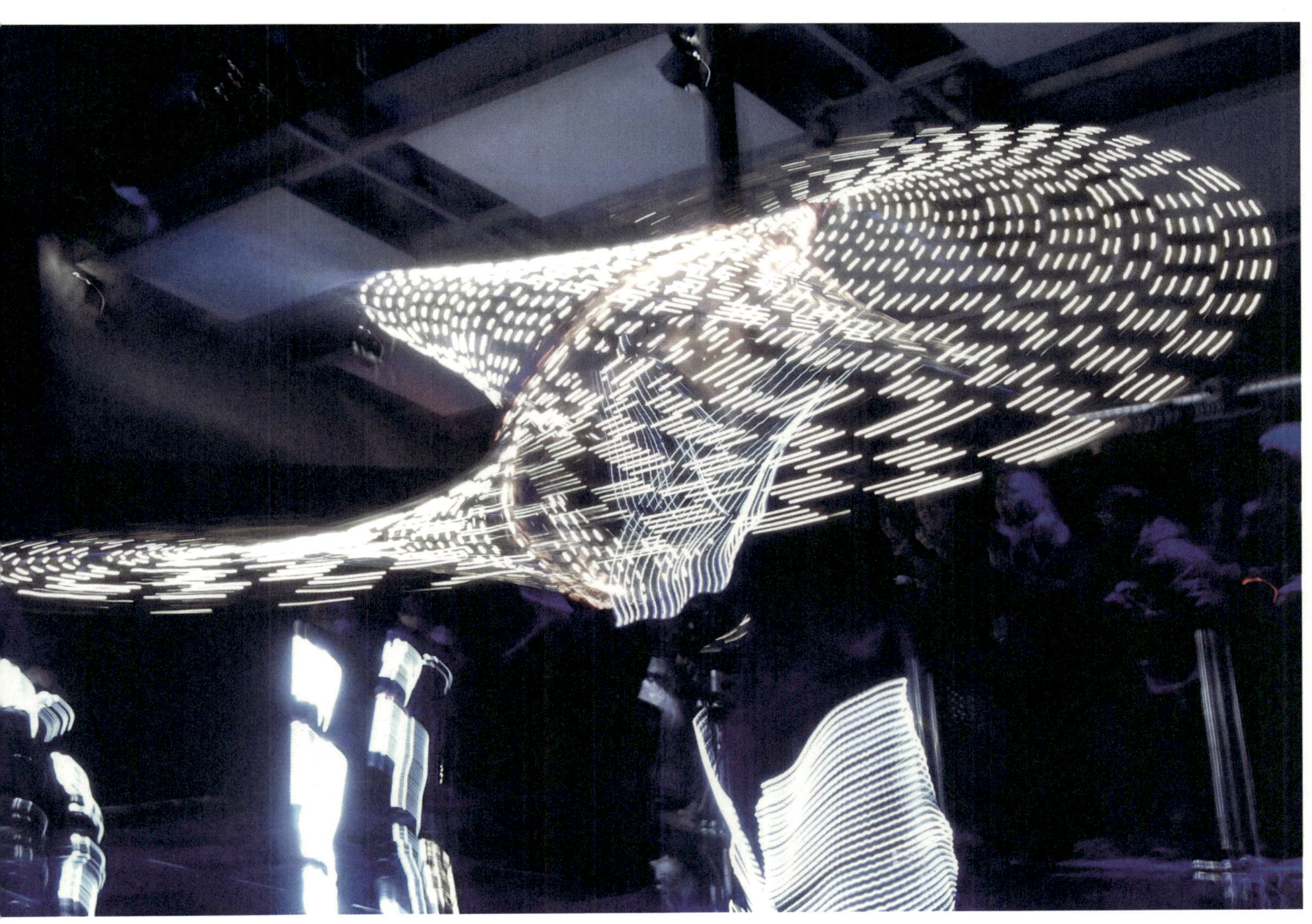

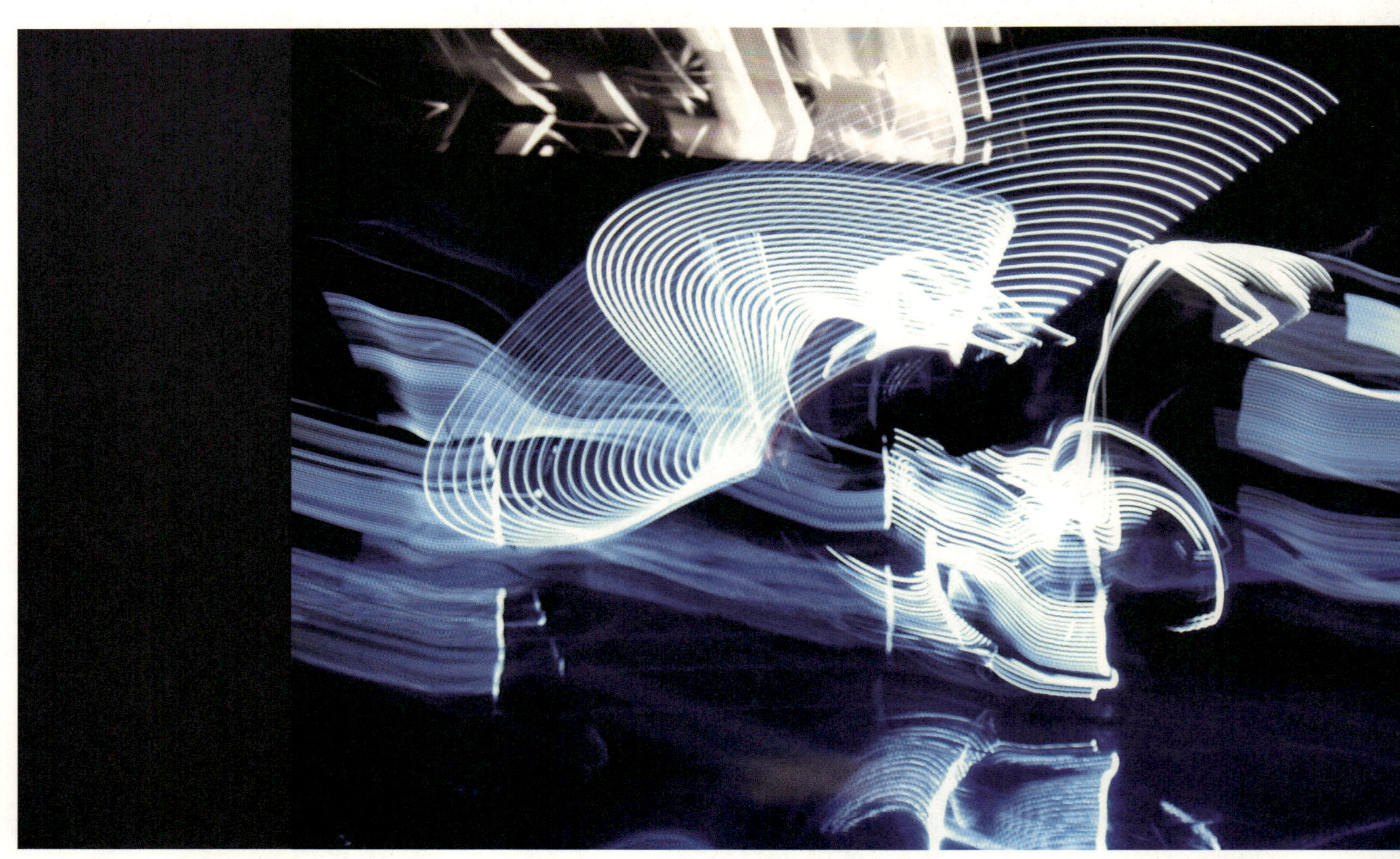

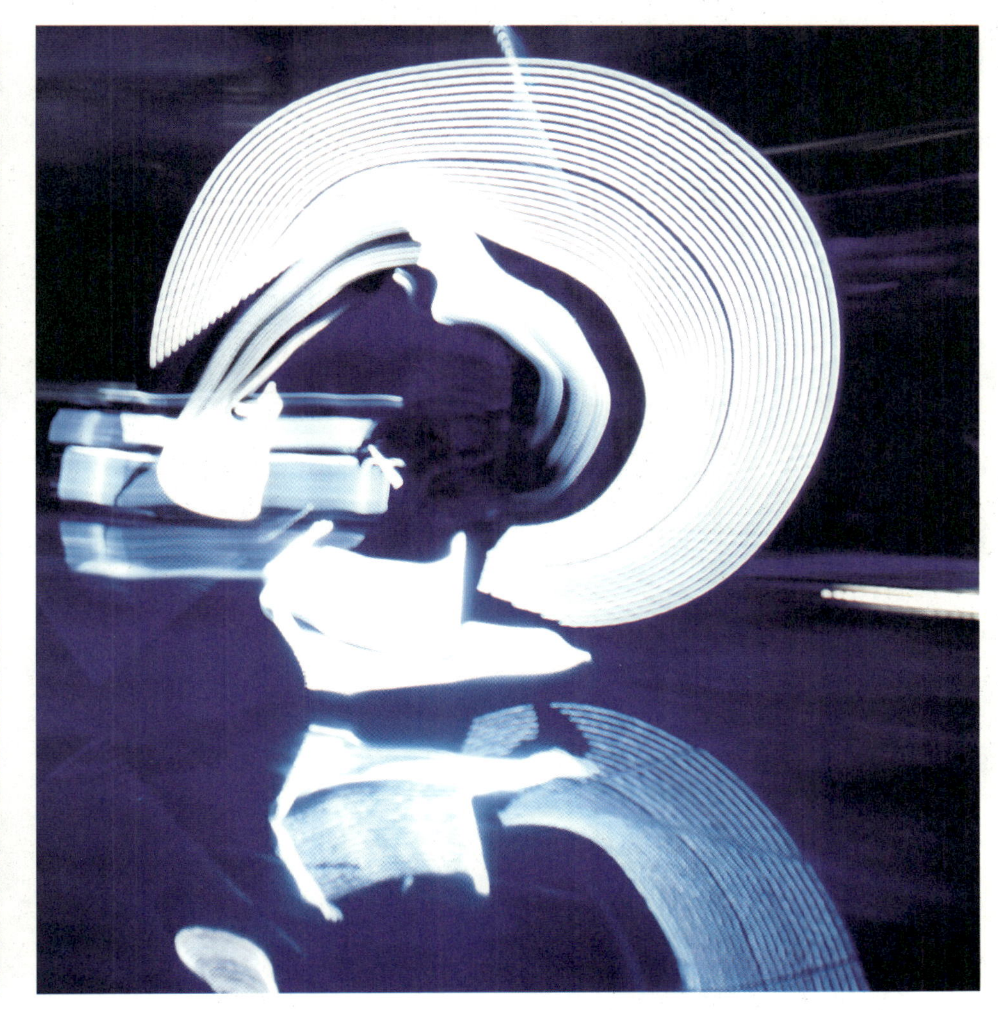

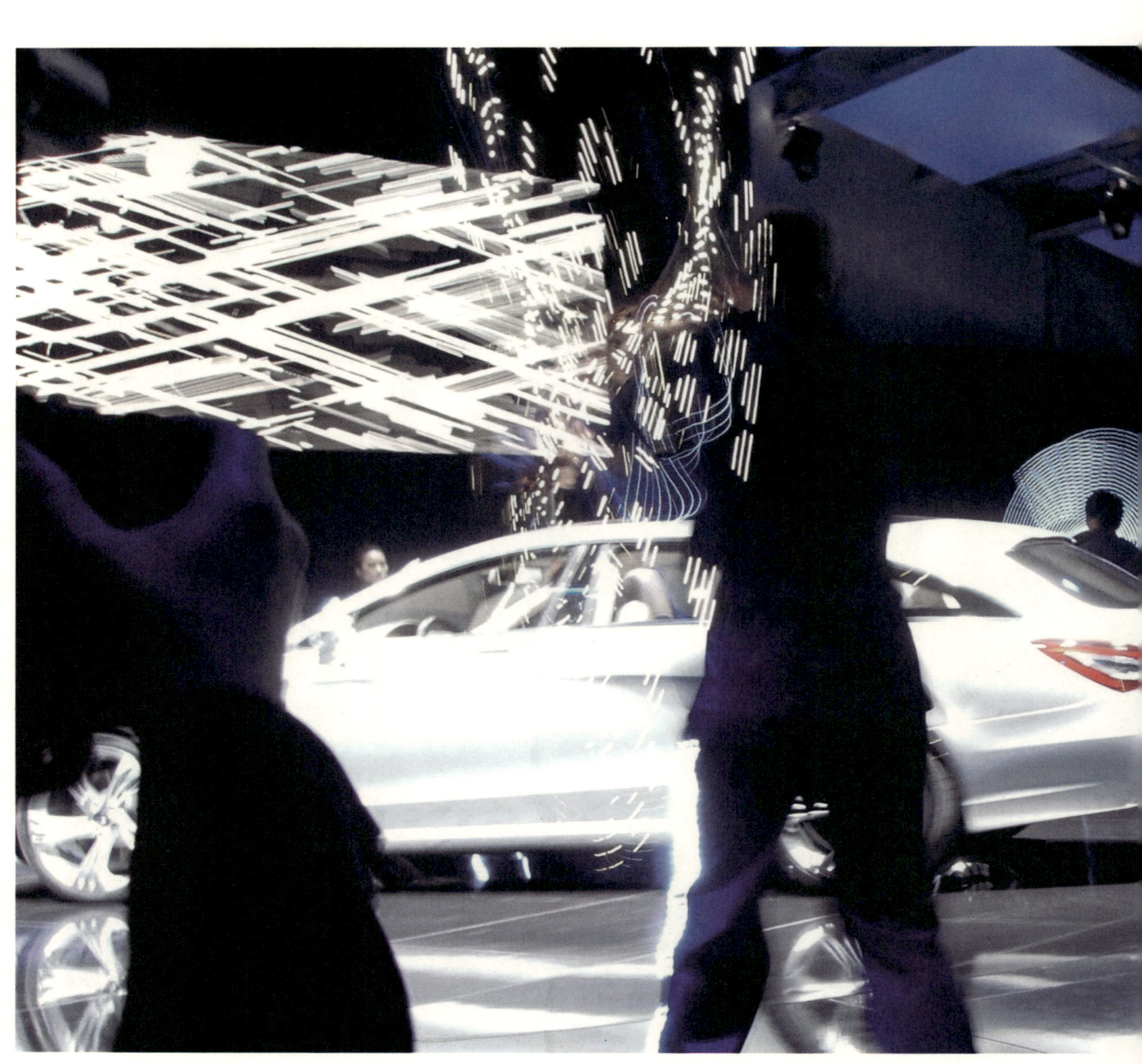

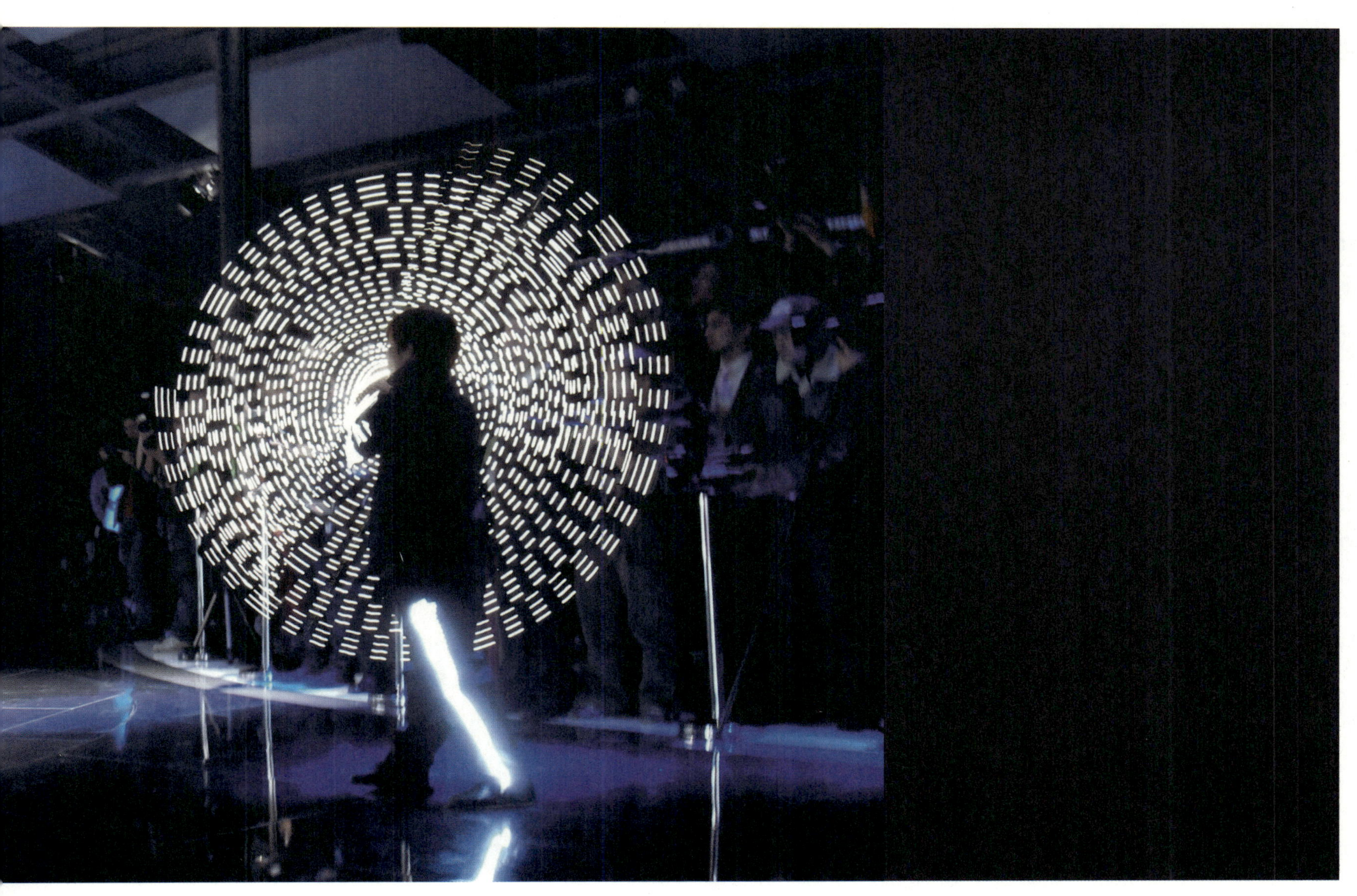

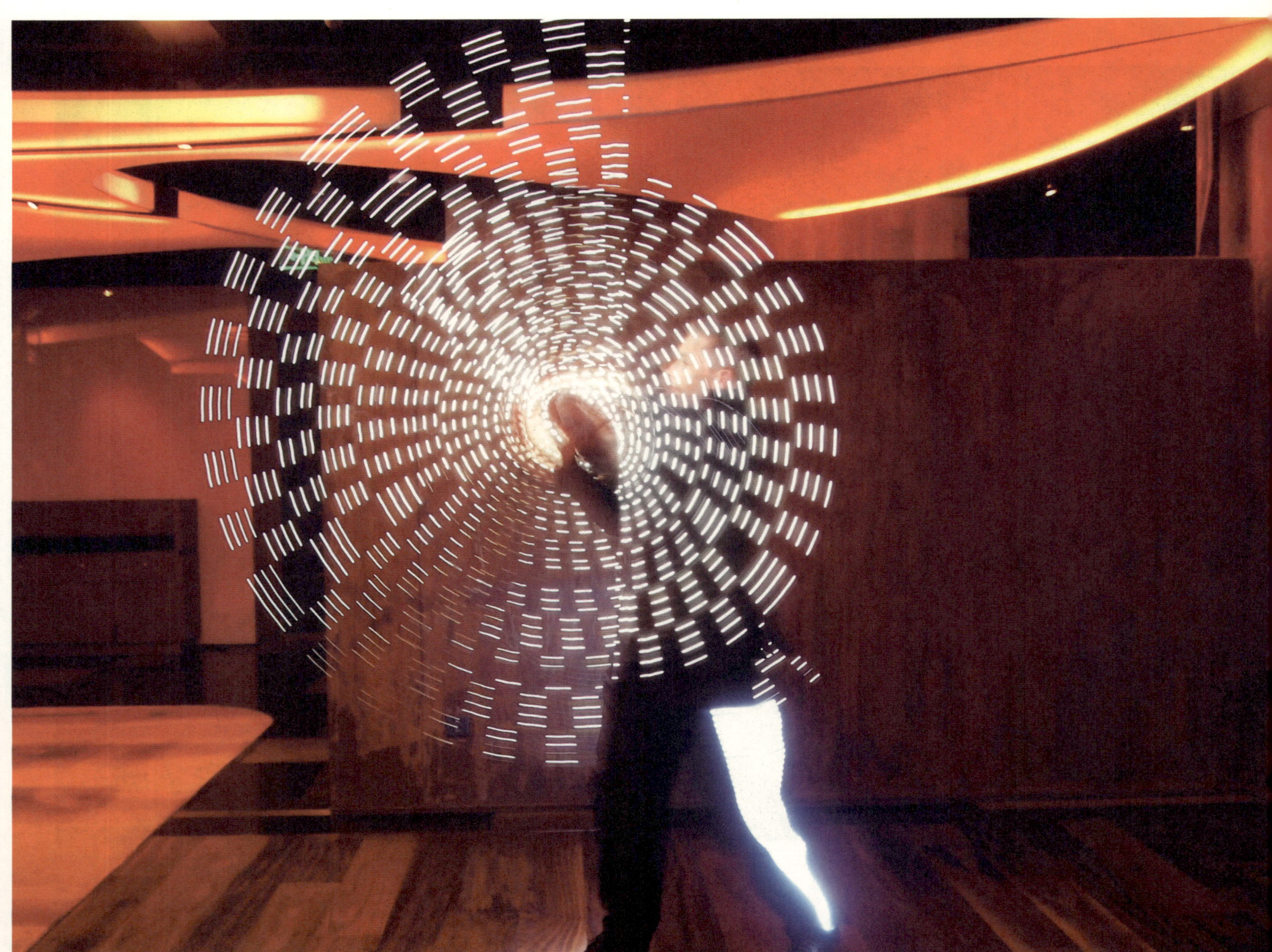

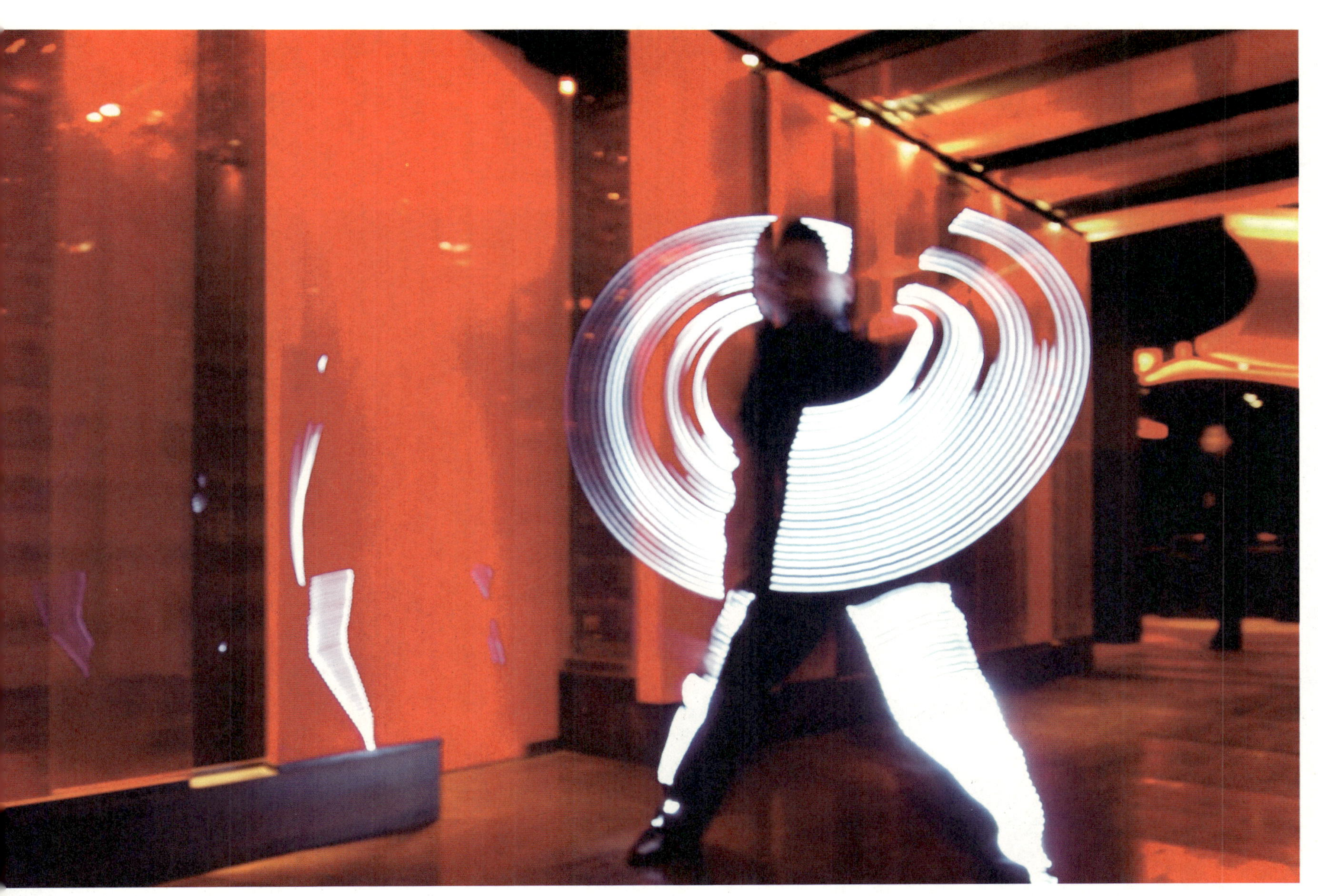

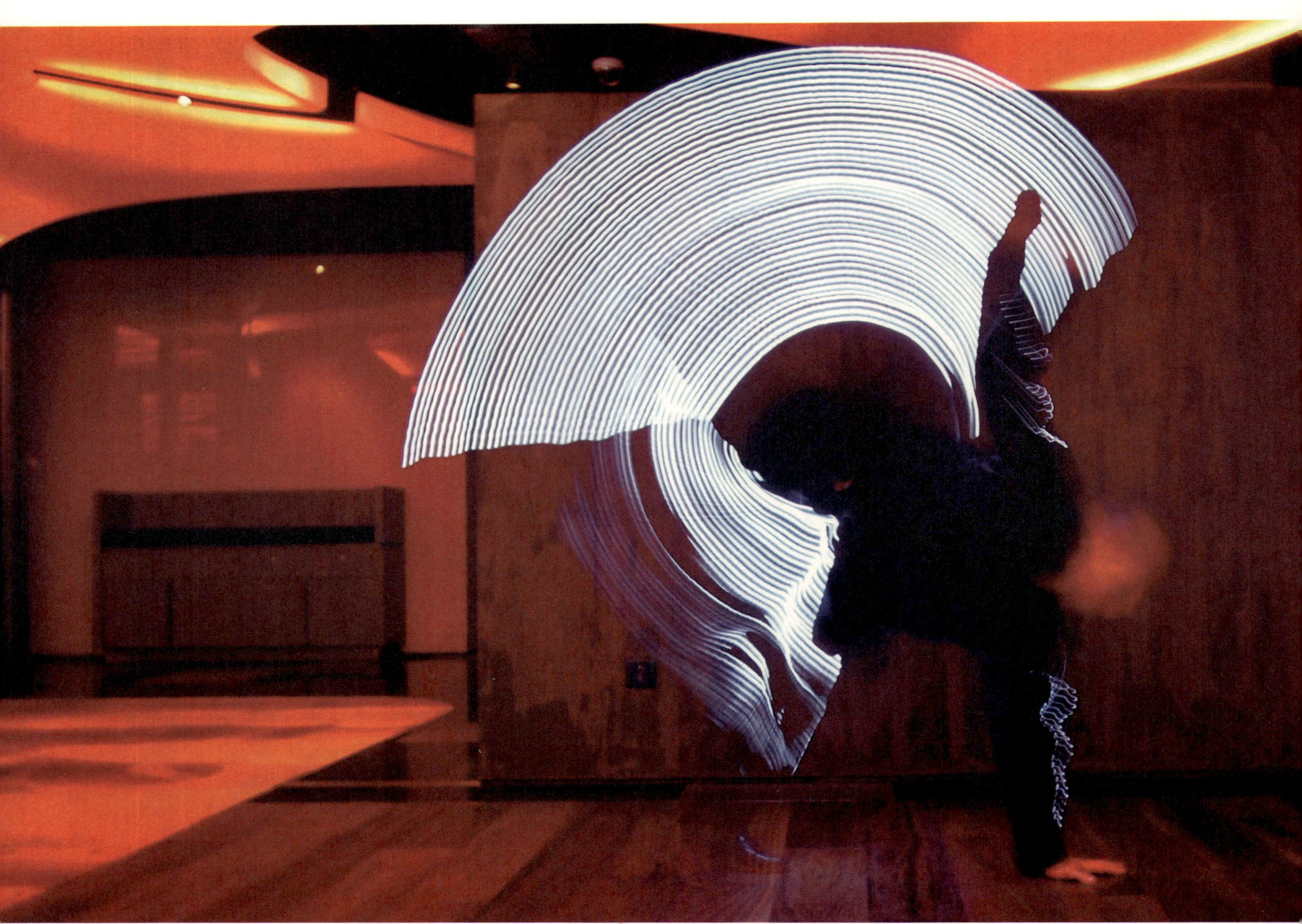

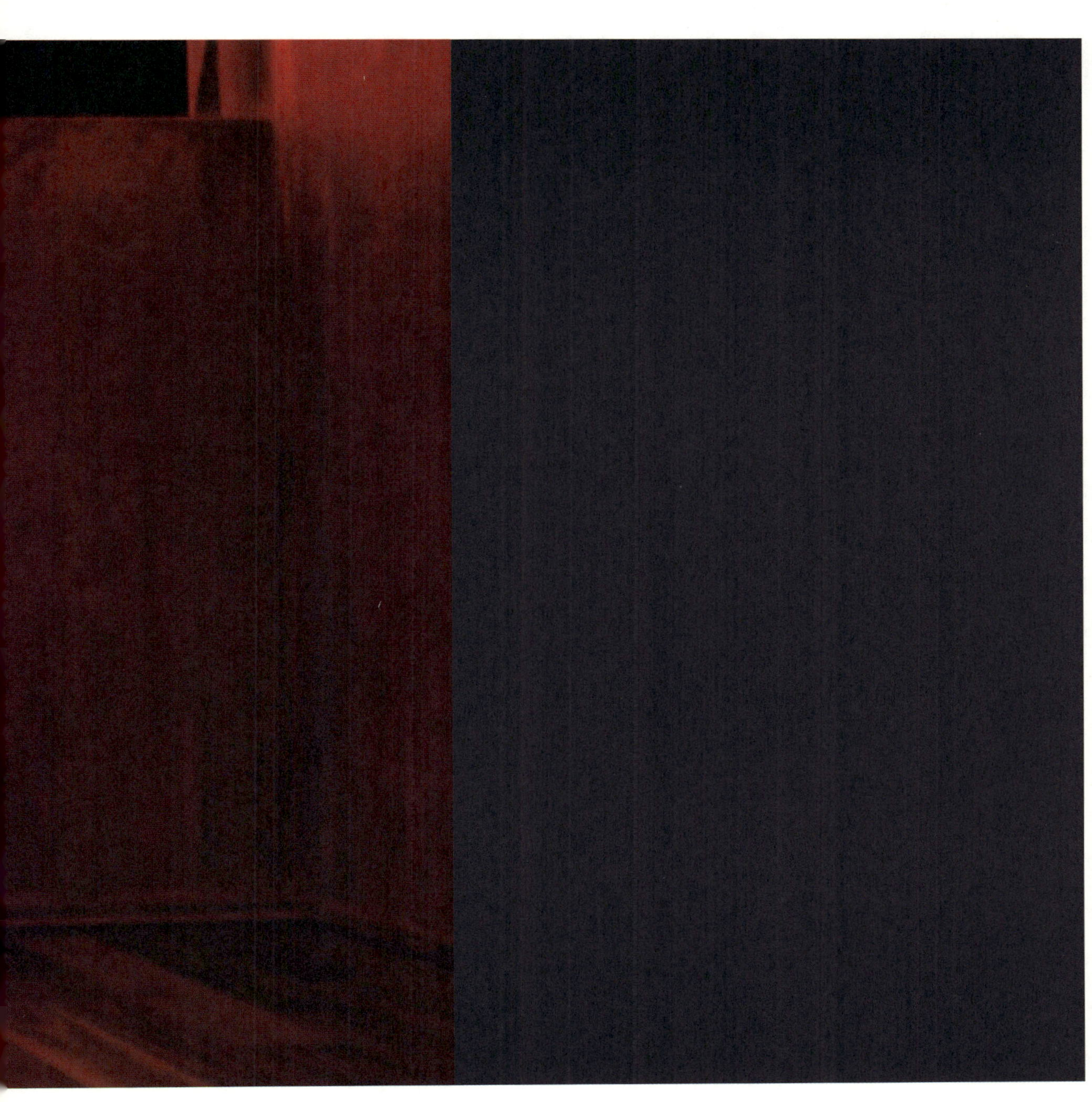

CHAMPAG

Following the success of the Mercedes-Benz performance, Moritz Waldemeyer was asked to create a scintillating martial arts extravaganza for the launch of Dom Pérignon's luminous label. Once again, Moritz enlisted the expertise of Martial arts choreographer Adam Rae. He was given Moritz's LED swords, programmed to write Dom Pérignon or to display their coat of arms when waved through the air. The performers worked together to create an all-girl, post-apocalyptic, Charlie's Angels pastiche – light-hearted as well as light-driven - playing on the 'Champagne girls' of the VIP club scene who accompany an expensive bottle purchase. Here, three of the world's top female martial artists, Selina Lo, Cecily Fay and Lizzie Gough, were transported into the future with light-emitting weapons, LED-embellished outfits, and the dramatic backdrop of One Mayfair. After dinner, Moritz and his team decided to mess about with the weapons in London. You can see them playing around with the iconic British Museum lion statues, creating luminous manes for them, or mystical swirls. These experiments were soon put to an end by a disgruntled security guard. Such moments, spontaneous and opportunistic, encapsulate Moritz's playful approach to the making of art.

Moritz was next invited to participate in ModaFad's grand annual fashion show. ModaFad exhibits Spain's best two new fashion designer talents, providing a prestigious forum for their work. Its focus on the next generation of fashion joins seamlessly with Moritz's futuristic approach. The show took place at Fàbrica Moritz, a nineteenth century brewery of Moritz beer – "I felt it was calling to me, calling my name!" he remembers - restored by French architect Jean Nouvel. Nouvel modernised the structure of the building but conserved the original brickwork and wax-treated beer tanks leaving an architectural treasure trove full of quirky recesses and unique textures. At the show, Moritz's dream team of Rae, Coleman, and Chloe Bruce wowed the audience with a live performance showing off their expert swordsmanship and full colour LED weapons. Aside from the performance, Moritz and Adam explored the dark catacombs of the ancient brewery seeking dynamic compositions that would develop the relationship between the space, weapon, and performer:

"WE HAD TO SEIZE THE MOMENT – IT WAS TOO PERFECT. WE BEGAN TO PLAY WITH THE ARCHITECTURE AND THE STRANGE QUALITY OF THE BREWERY WALLS. I ENLISTED SOME MODELS AND HAD THEM POSE WHILE A MARTIAL ARTIST CARVED OUT AN IMAGE IN THE AIR. IN ONE SHOT, I LOVE HOW THE WINGED SILHOUETTE OF THE BAT GRAPHIC ECHOES THE EAGLE EMBLEM ON THE MODEL'S SKIRT – IT WAS A SURPRISE I ONLY SAW WHEN LOOKING OVER THE PHOTOS AGAIN."

When Camron, the design communications agency based in London and New York, were looking for an original Christmas card, they commissioned Moritz Waldemeyer to create a London-inspired light painting. The successful Olympic bid led him to enrol UK gymnast, Hasit Savani to perform with an LED prop at various iconic locations along the South Bank. Moritz designed a winter-themed snowflake graphic that would trace the movements of the gymnast as he performed.

NE SUPERNOVA

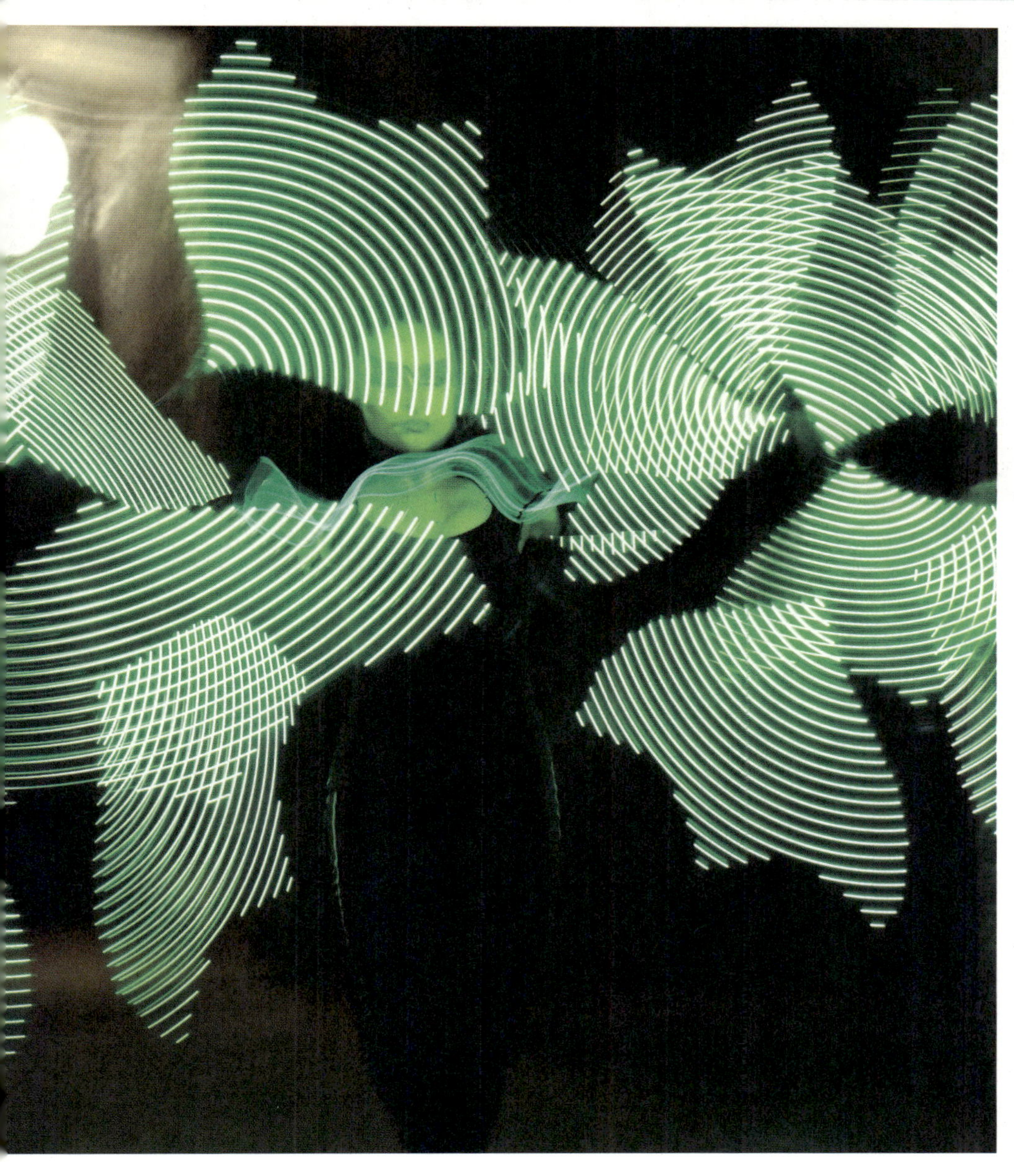

Later on in this chapter, you can see the ethereal snowflakes seemingly blown in delicate gusts, the effect paradoxically created through the powerful flips and rolls of the gymnast. In the National Theatre shot, the long exposure works particularly well with the brief: the modern architecture and lighting of the theatre are echoed by the light painting's colouring. The red and yellow strokes behind the graphic are from the iconic double decker bus, whilst the most famous landmark in London, St. Pauls Cathedral, shines through bus and graphic triumphantly.

Having developed a full colour version of the sword, Moritz wanted to experiment with martial artists once again. Finally, we see the results of an experimental photo-shoot taken in the Commonwealth Institute, shortly before its renovation into the new London Design Museum. The combination of bright cartoon-like graphics, bold architectural lines and dramatic shadow play creates illustration-like images in real time.

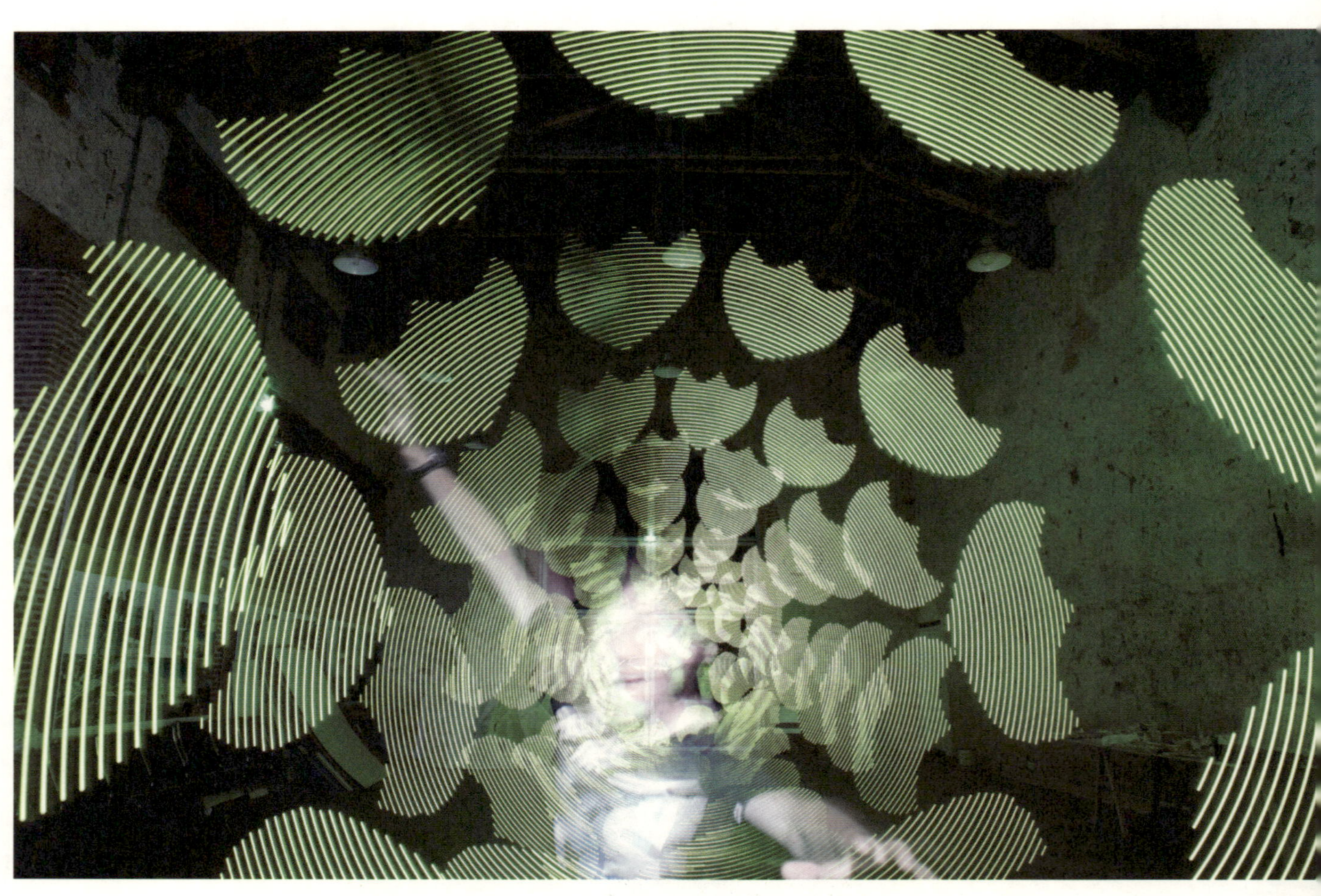

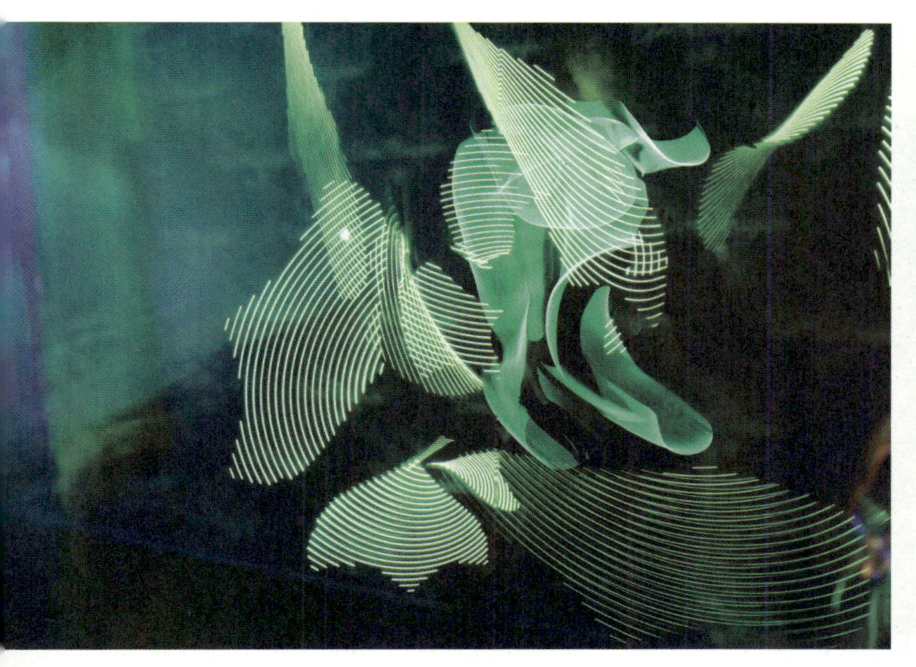

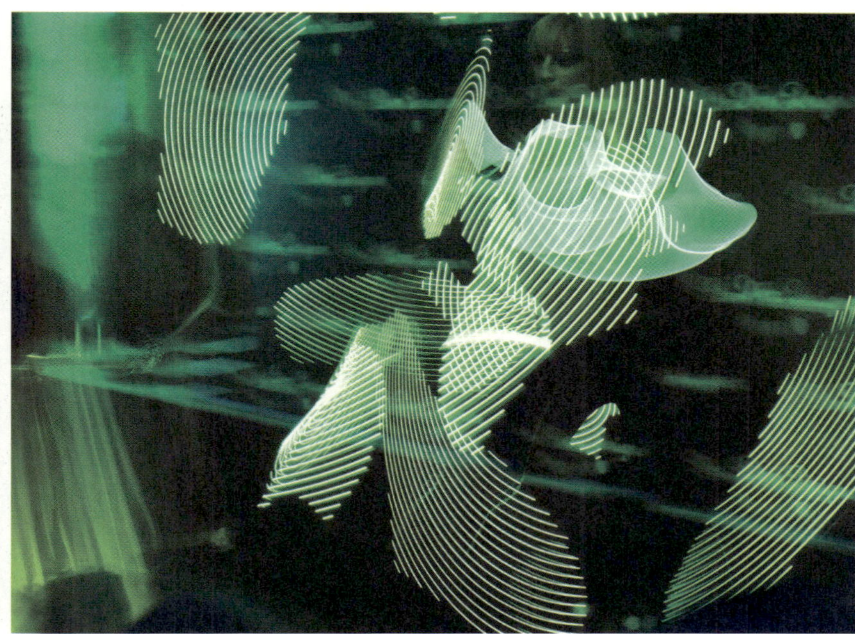

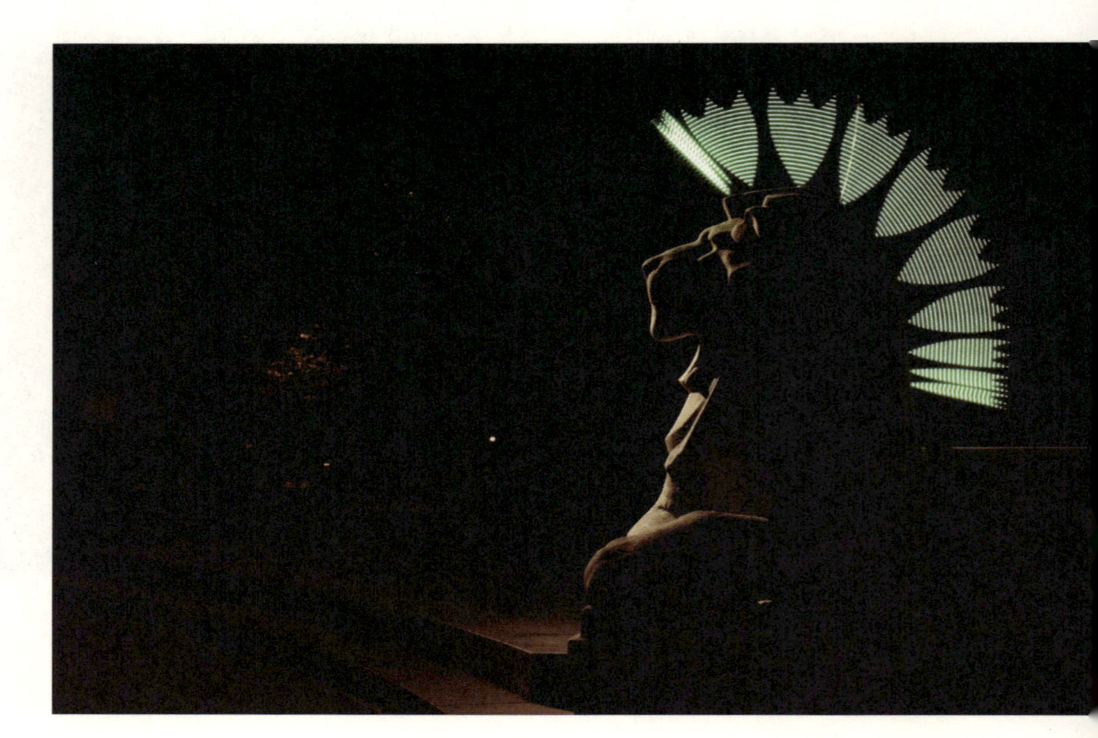

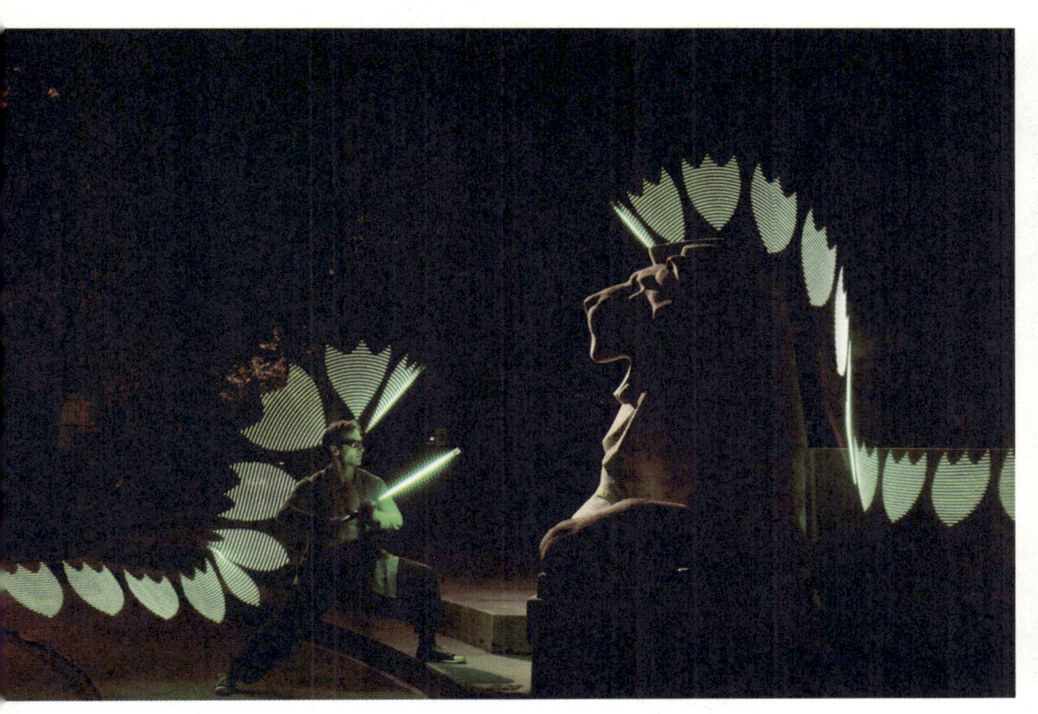

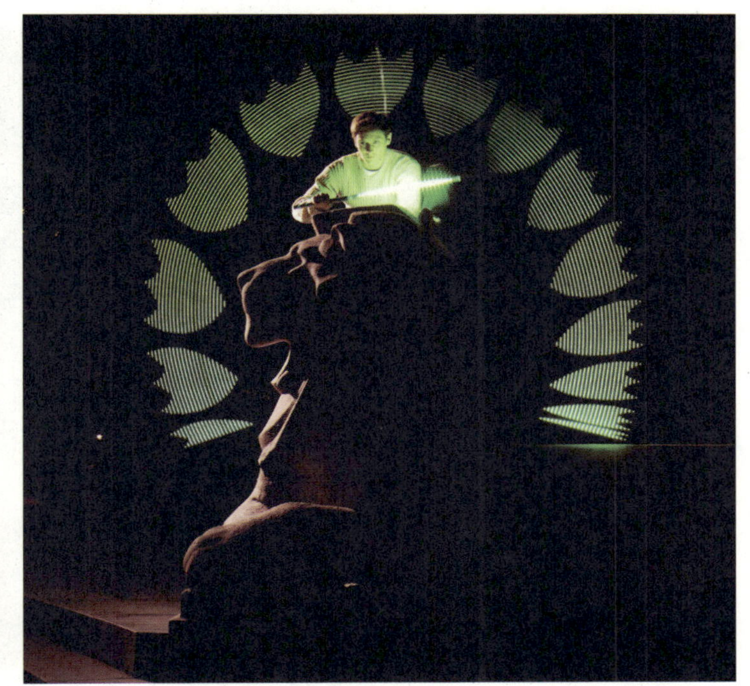

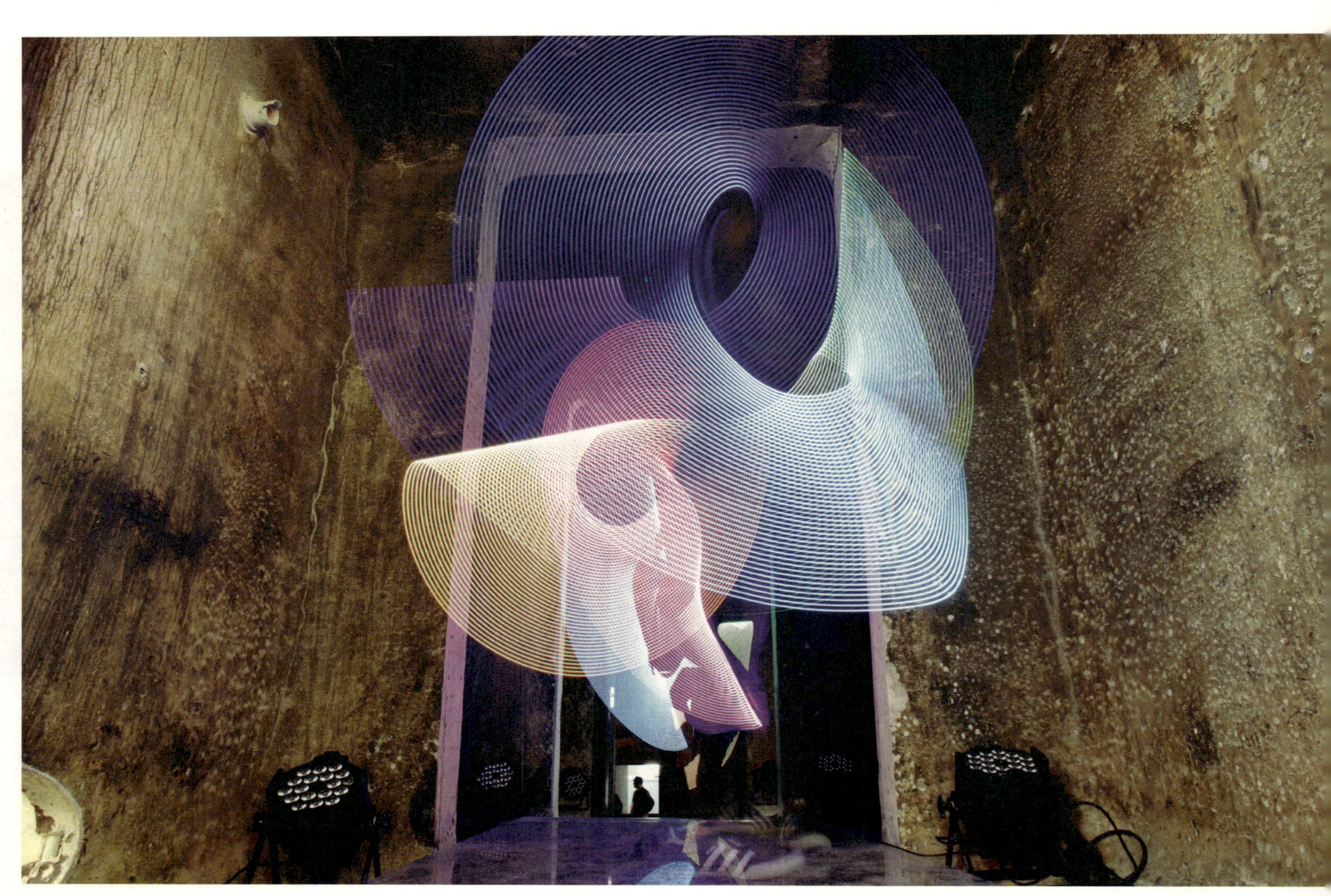

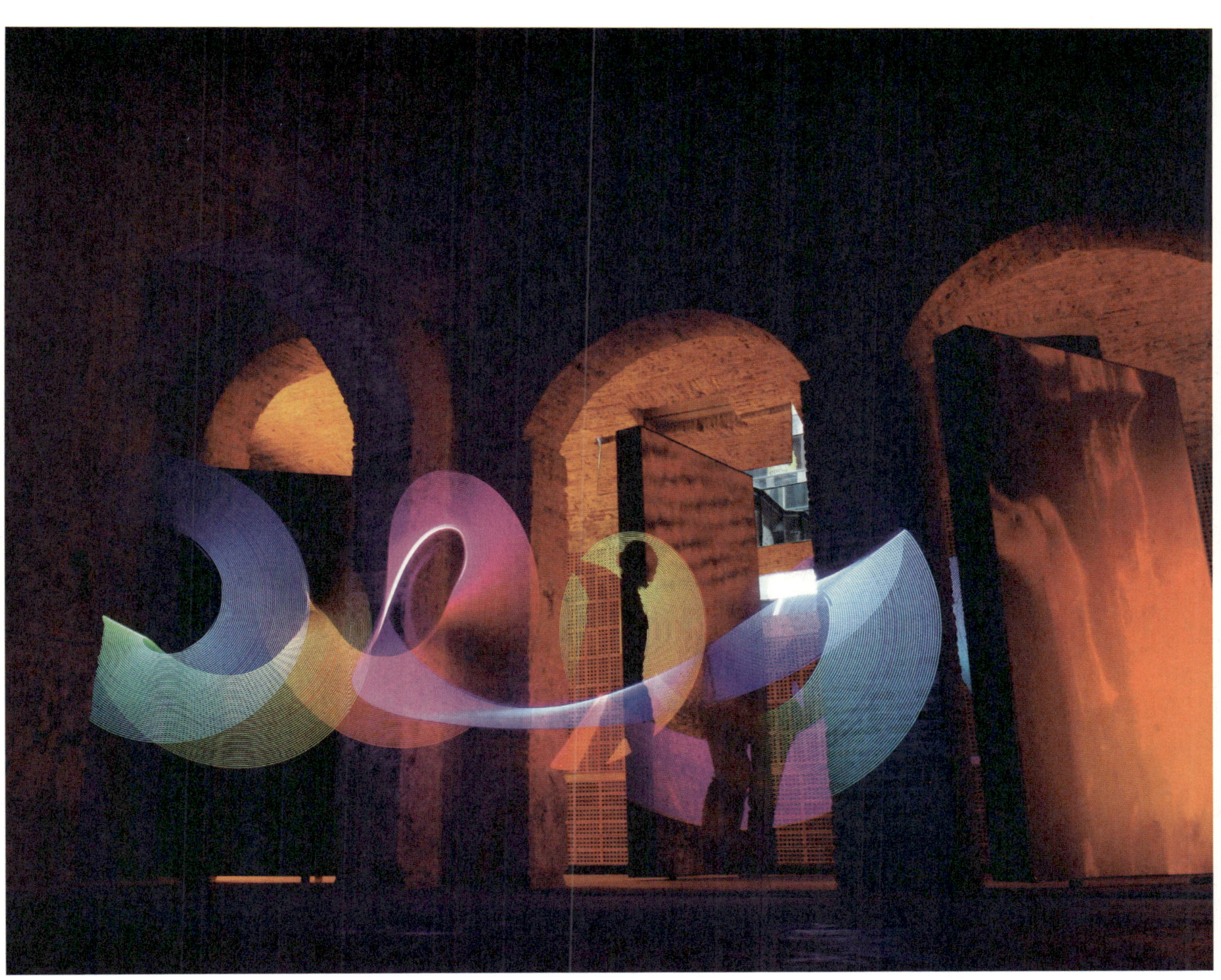

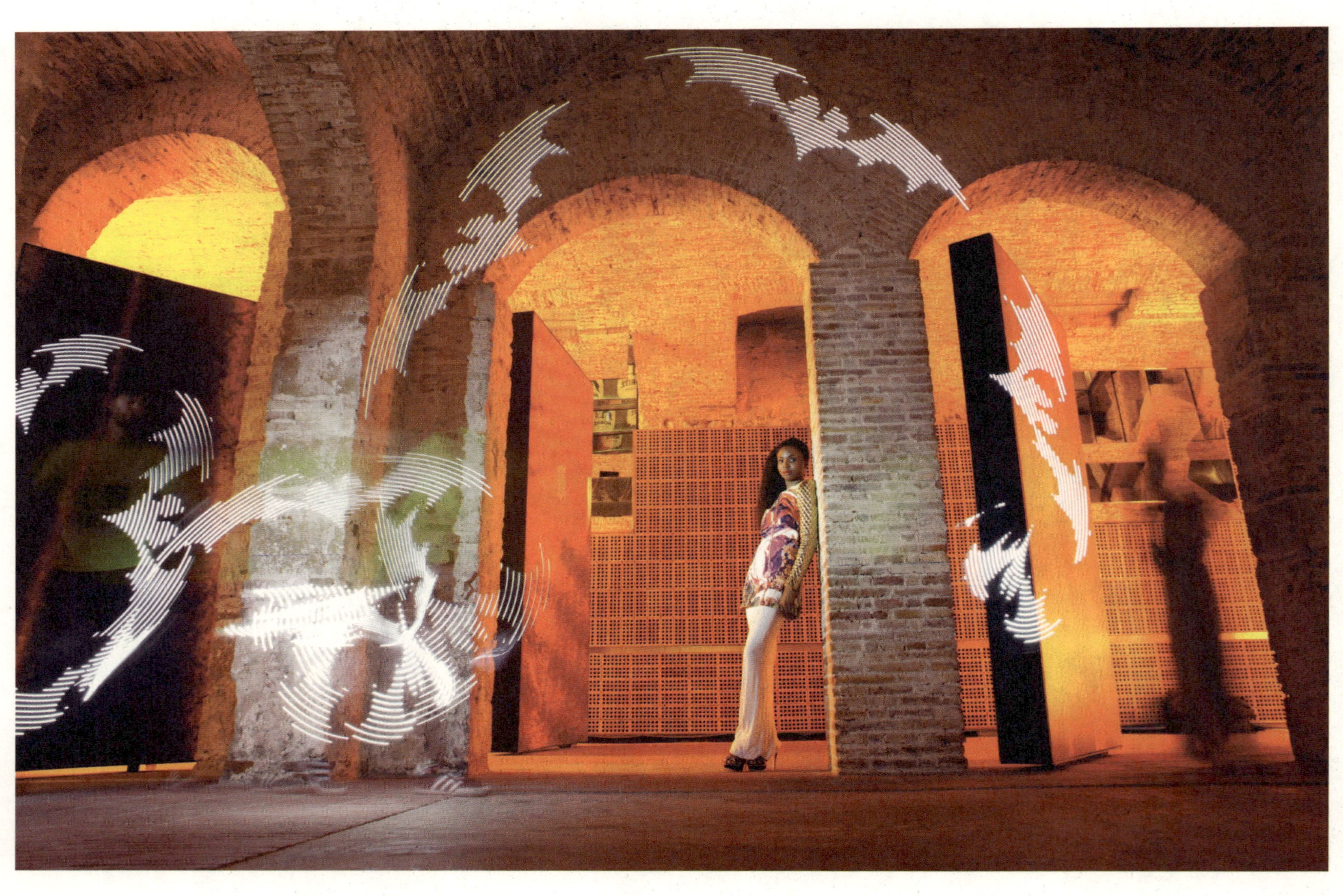

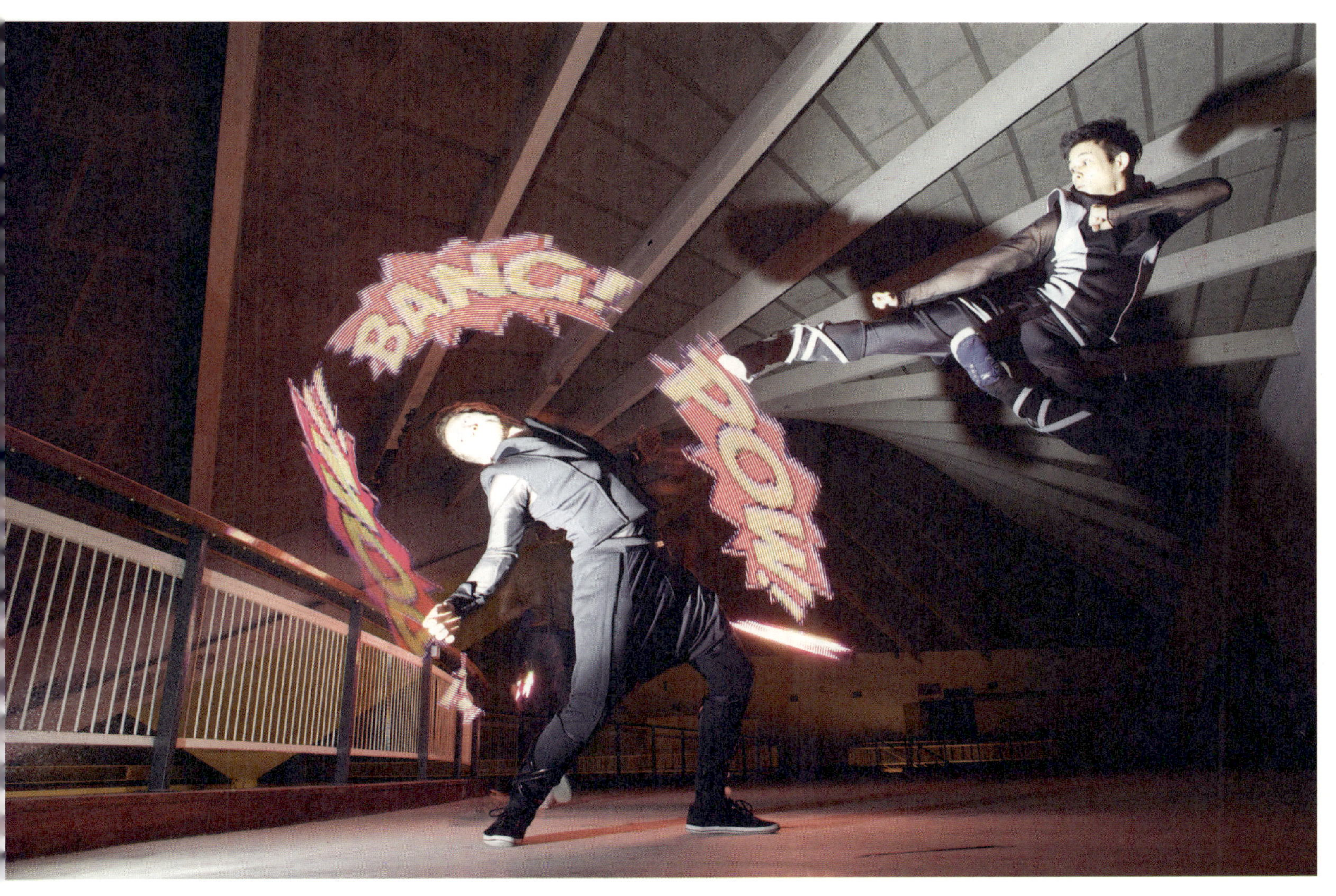
BANG!
POW!

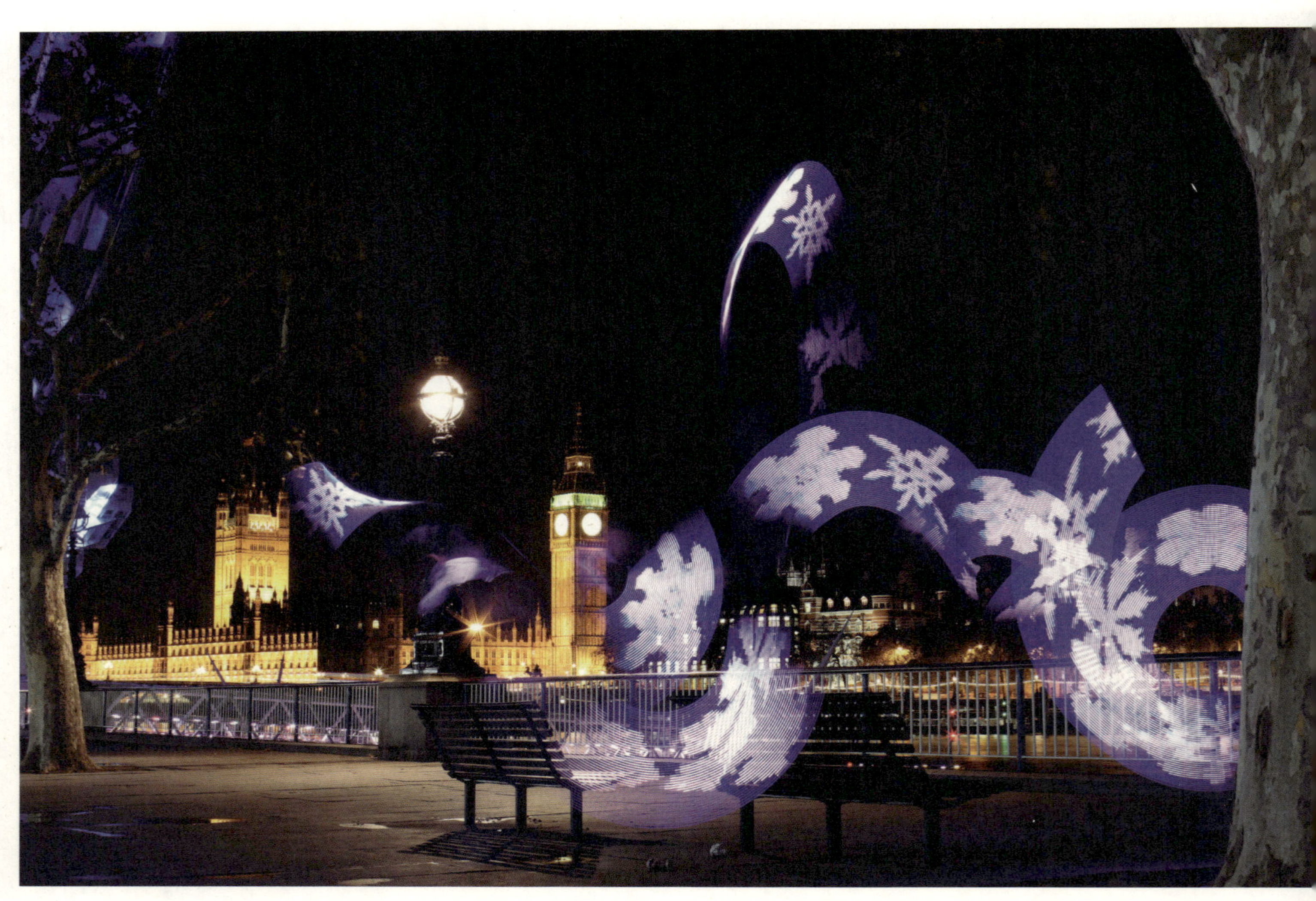

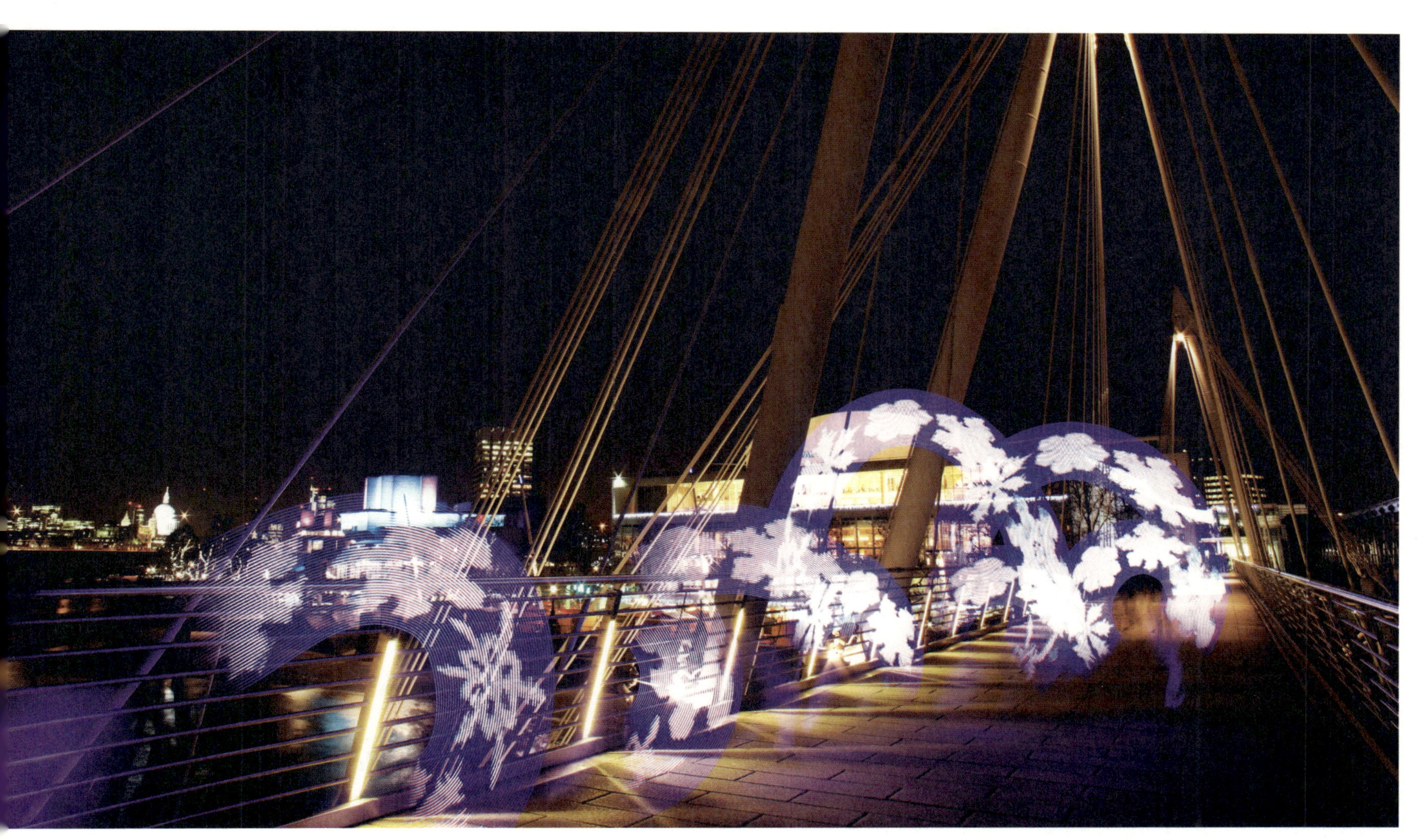

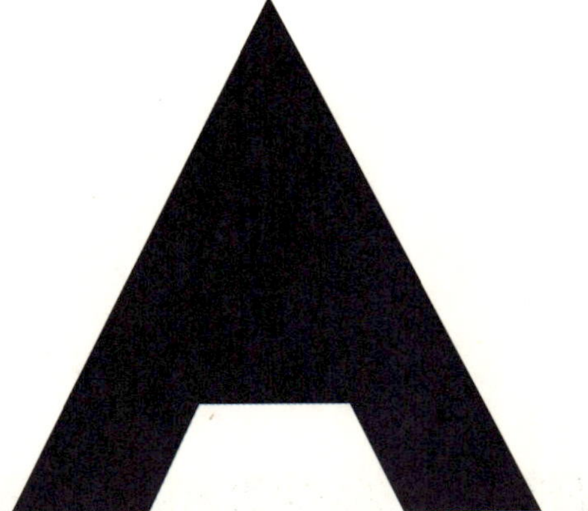

A NEW

A few months after Moritz Waldemeyer's first Mercedes-Benz collaboration, he was invited by Mercedes-Benz.com to create a film showcasing the new LED headlights of the Mercedes CLS, shot by fischerAppelt agency. Hoping to express the theatrical potential of painting with light through space, alongside the perfection of a single well-composed photograph, Moritz decided to bring the concept into the third dimension:

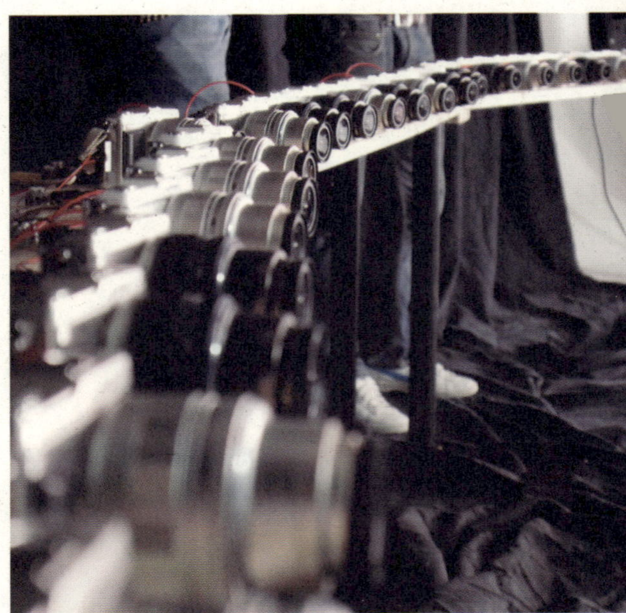

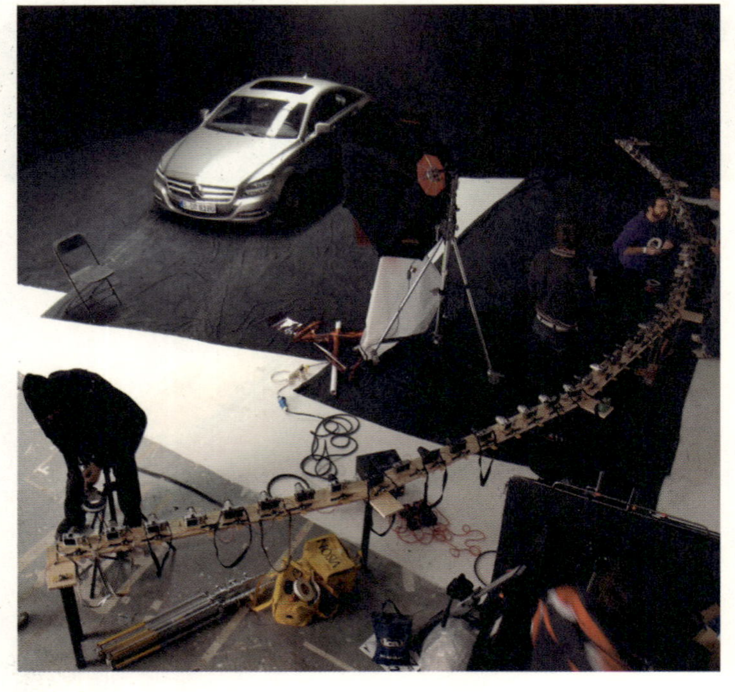

"WHEN WE TALK ABOUT PERFORMANCE ARTISTS LIKE BONO, RIHANNA OR KYLIE, IT'S ALWAYS ABOUT THE SHOW ON STAGE, IT'S ABOUT THE PERSON. BUT IN THIS CASE WE HAVE A CAR THAT WE WANT TO SHOW, SO WE USE LED OBJECTS WHICH WE MOVE IN A DANCE FIGHTING PERFORMANCE AND THROUGH THIS MOVEMENT, CREATE VIRTUAL LIGHT SCULPTURES."

V LIGHT

Camera maker Olympus agreed to loan out 50 cameras for the project that were arranged around a semi-circular rig. The cameras were programmed to take a long exposure photograph all at the same time, freezing the image from 50 different angles. The 3D effect is created by mounting all the images together in an animation so that the viewer has the effect of driving around the scene, from one camera to the next. The LED light traces left by the martial art performers, Rae, Coleman and Ismail, were captured as three-dimensional light sculptures for the first time. These patterns are complemented by the microcosmic interplay of lights on the reflective surface of the Mercedes. The very weapons themselves are designed to mirror the curved LEDs inside the headlight, which come together in the film. In the stills from this shoot we get a sense of the organic, orbit-like impressions left by the ferocious wushu manoeuvres. The interaction between ancient art and modern technology creates its own paradox between violent action and serene, natural form.

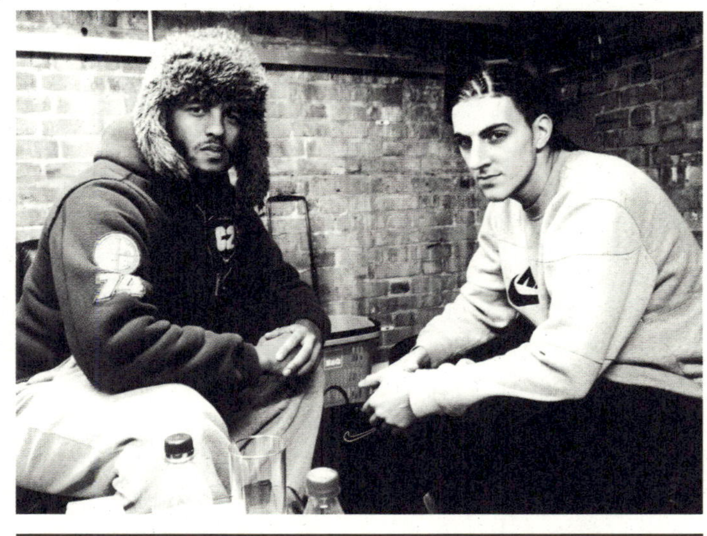

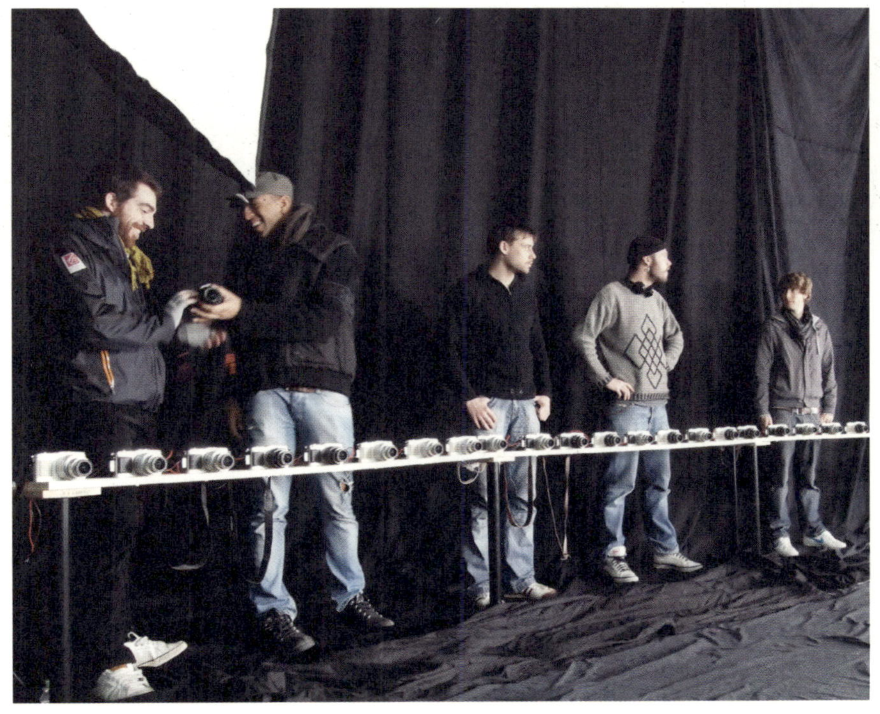

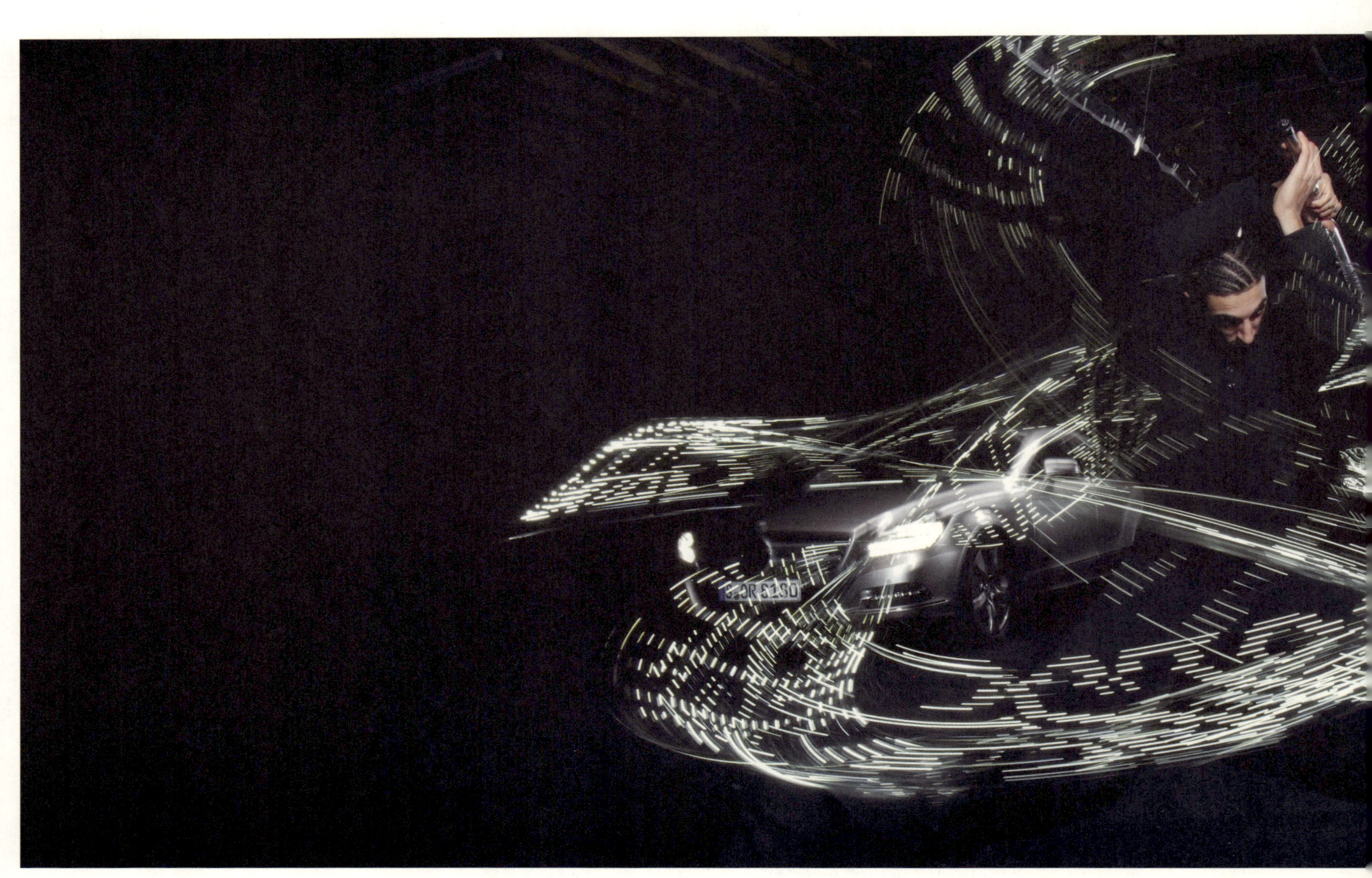

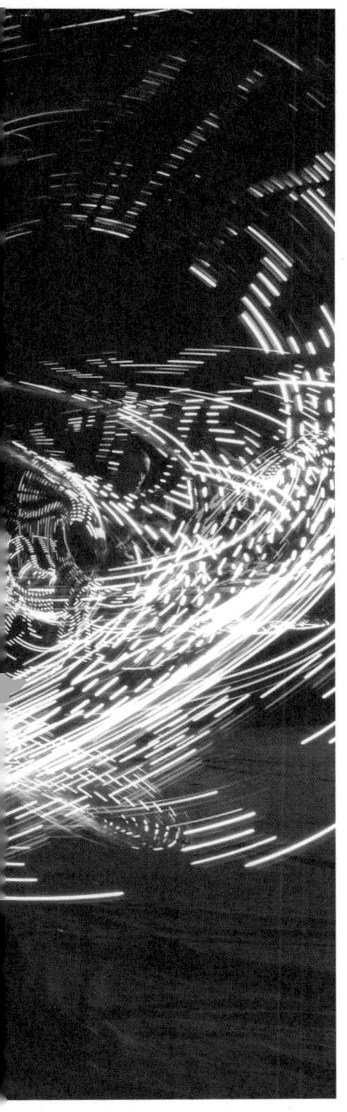

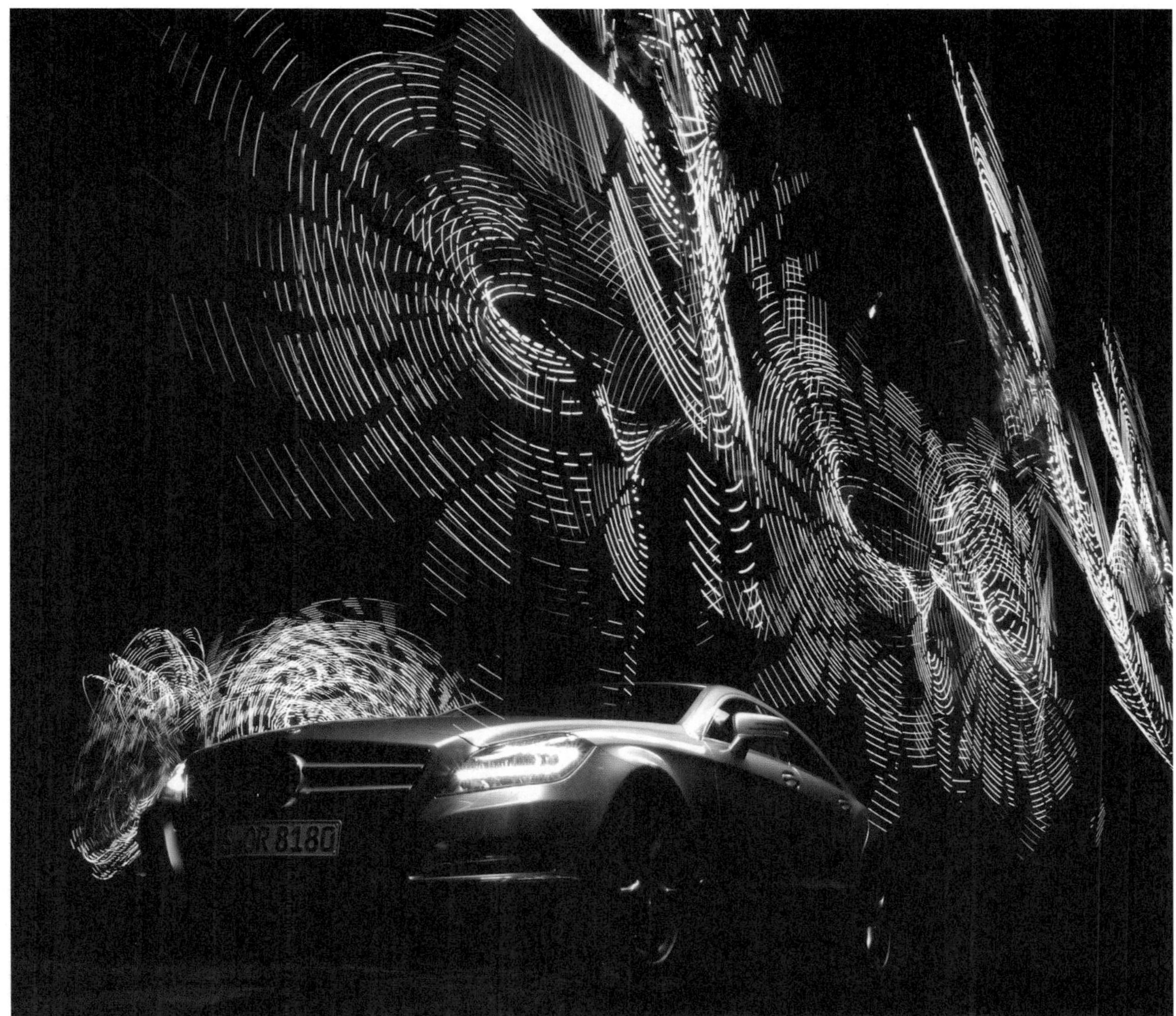

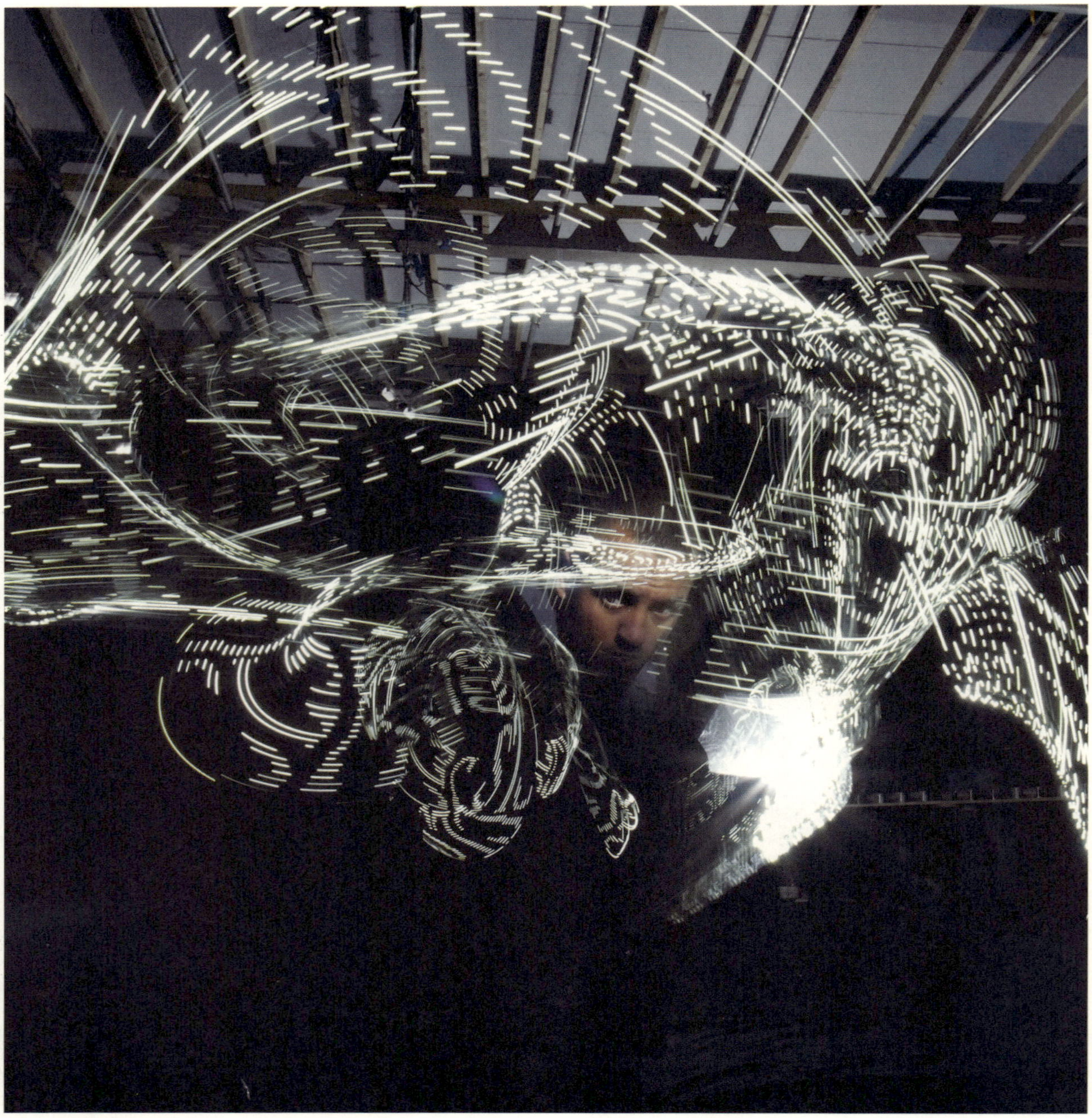

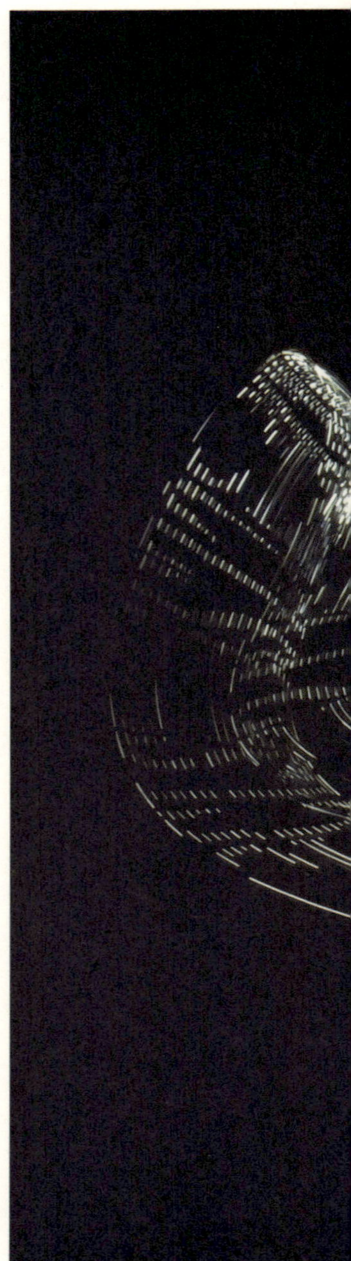

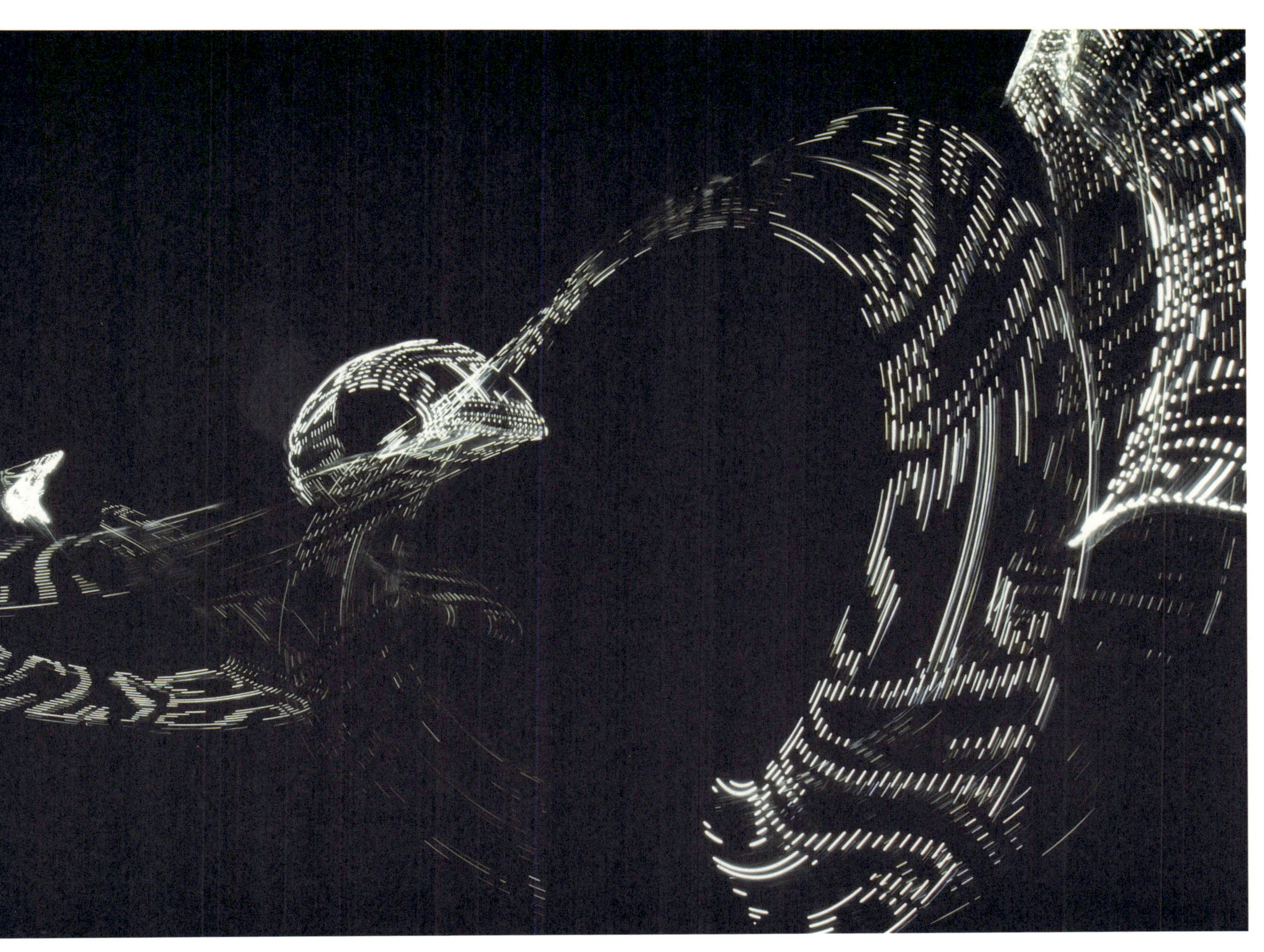

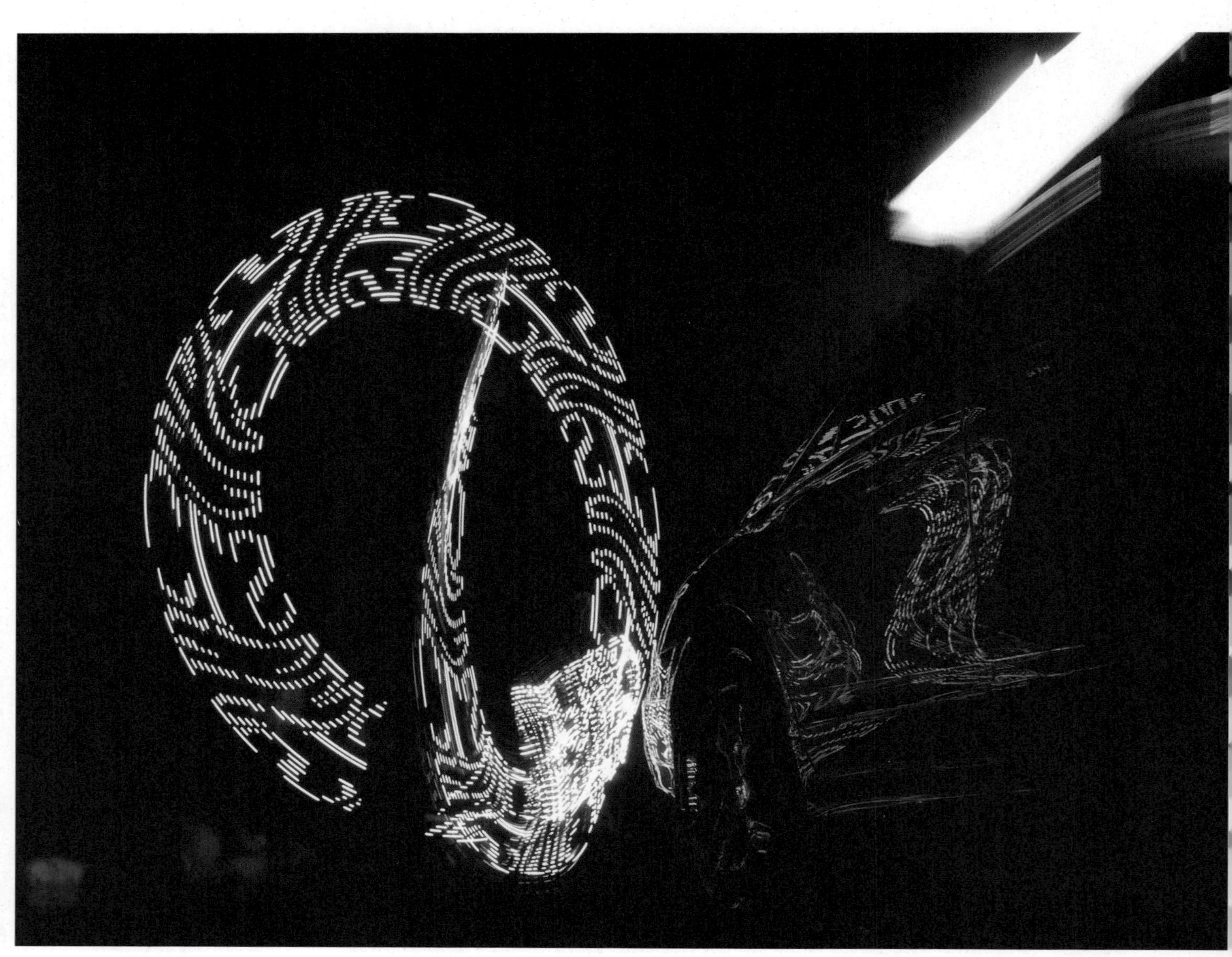

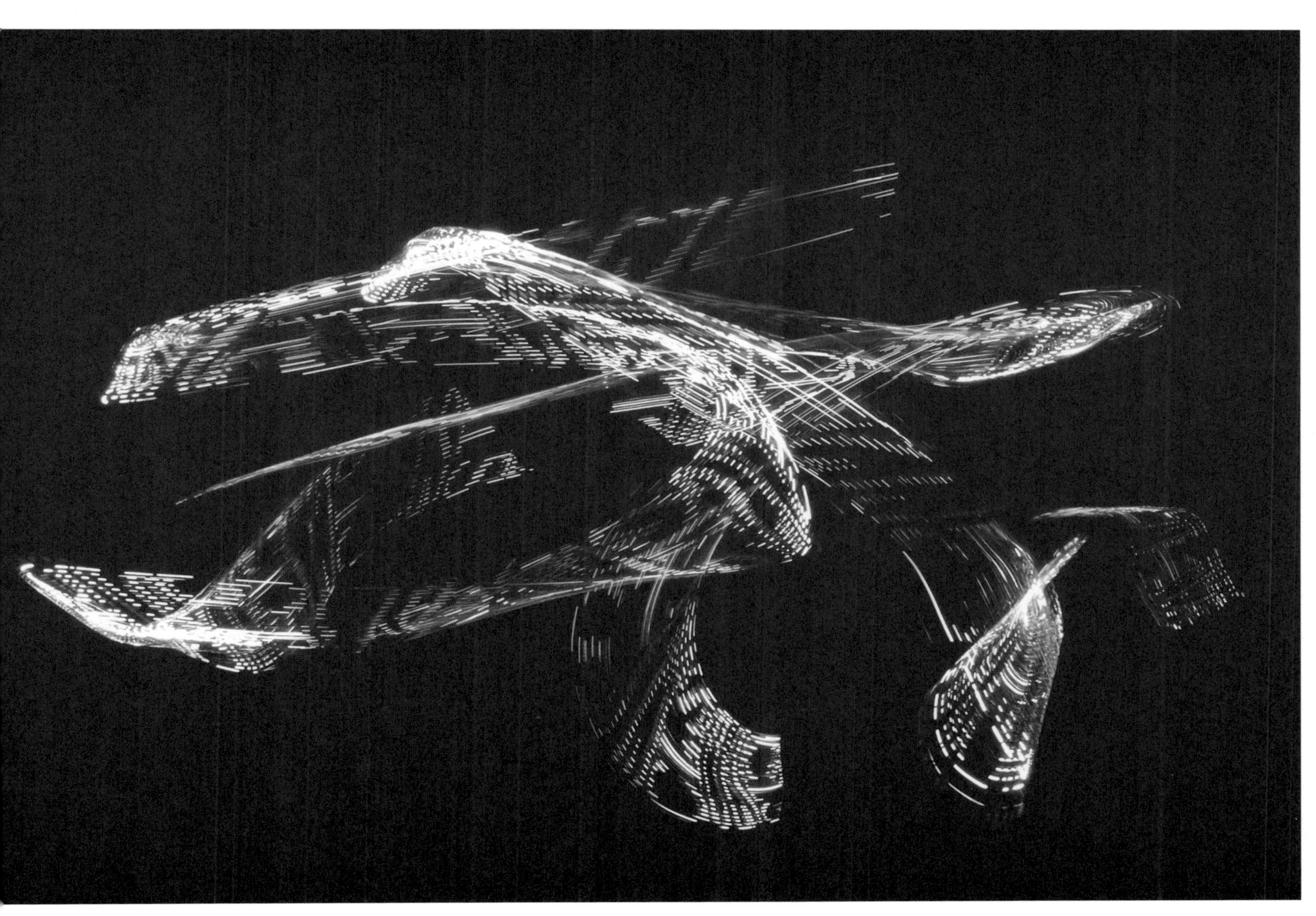

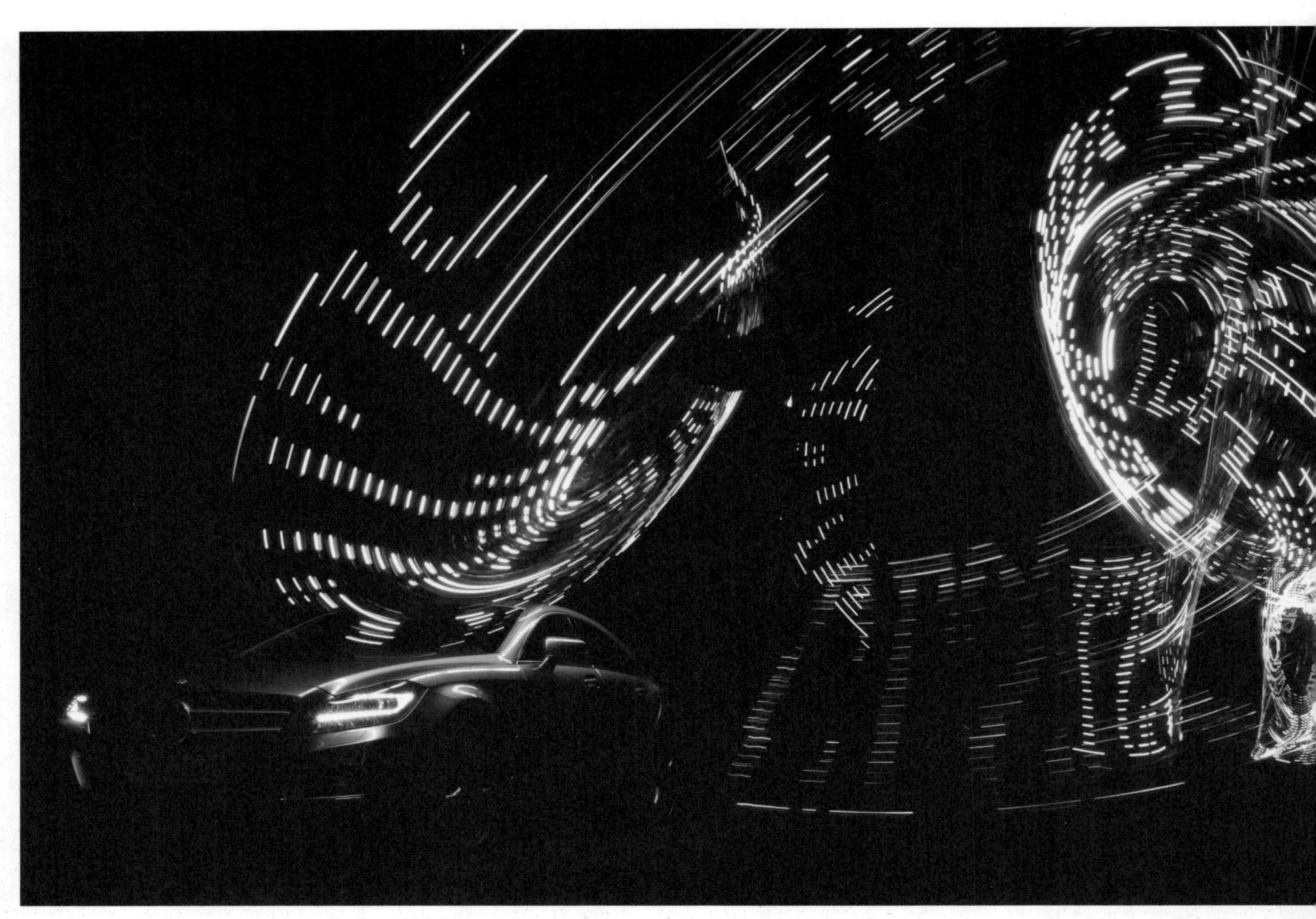

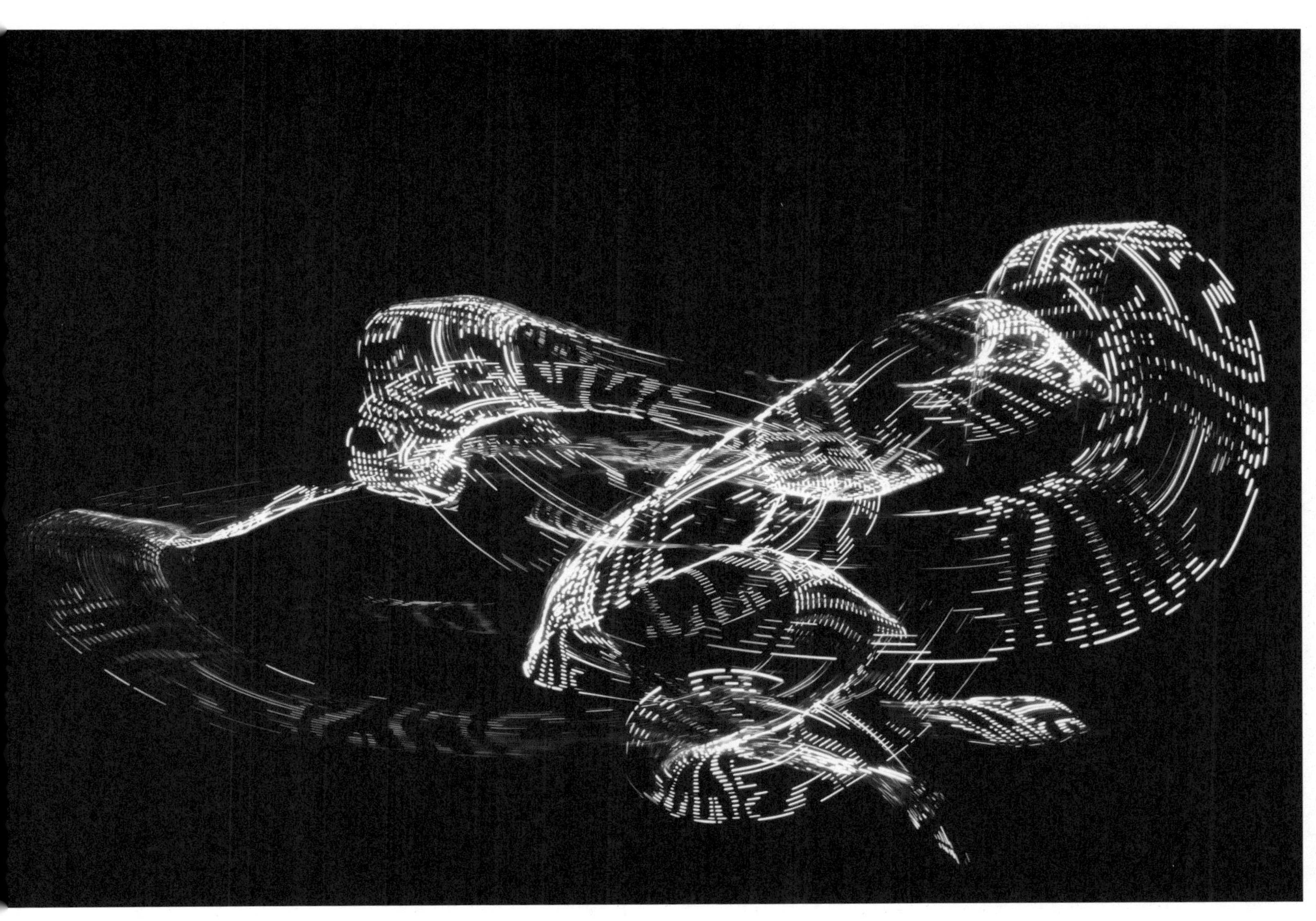

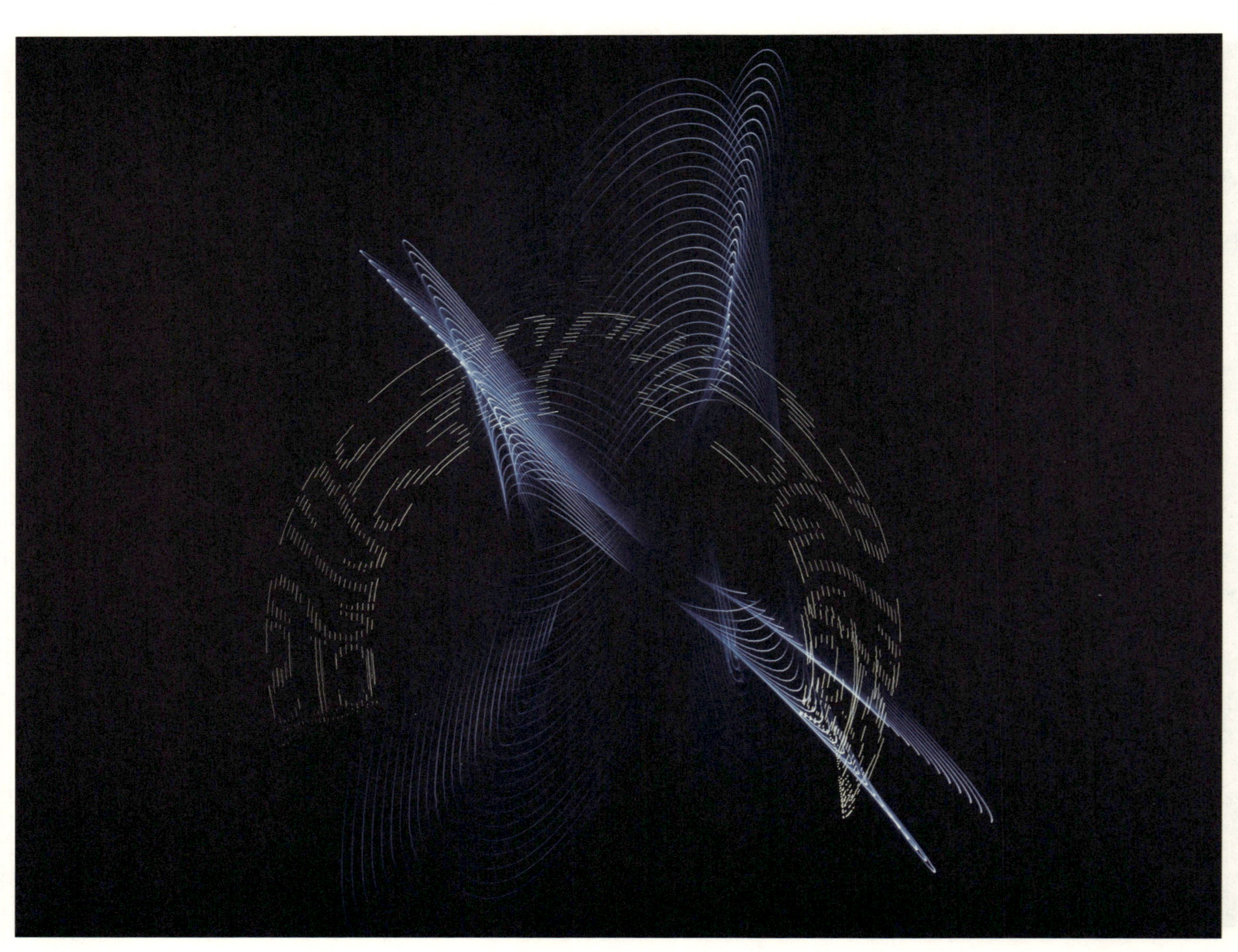

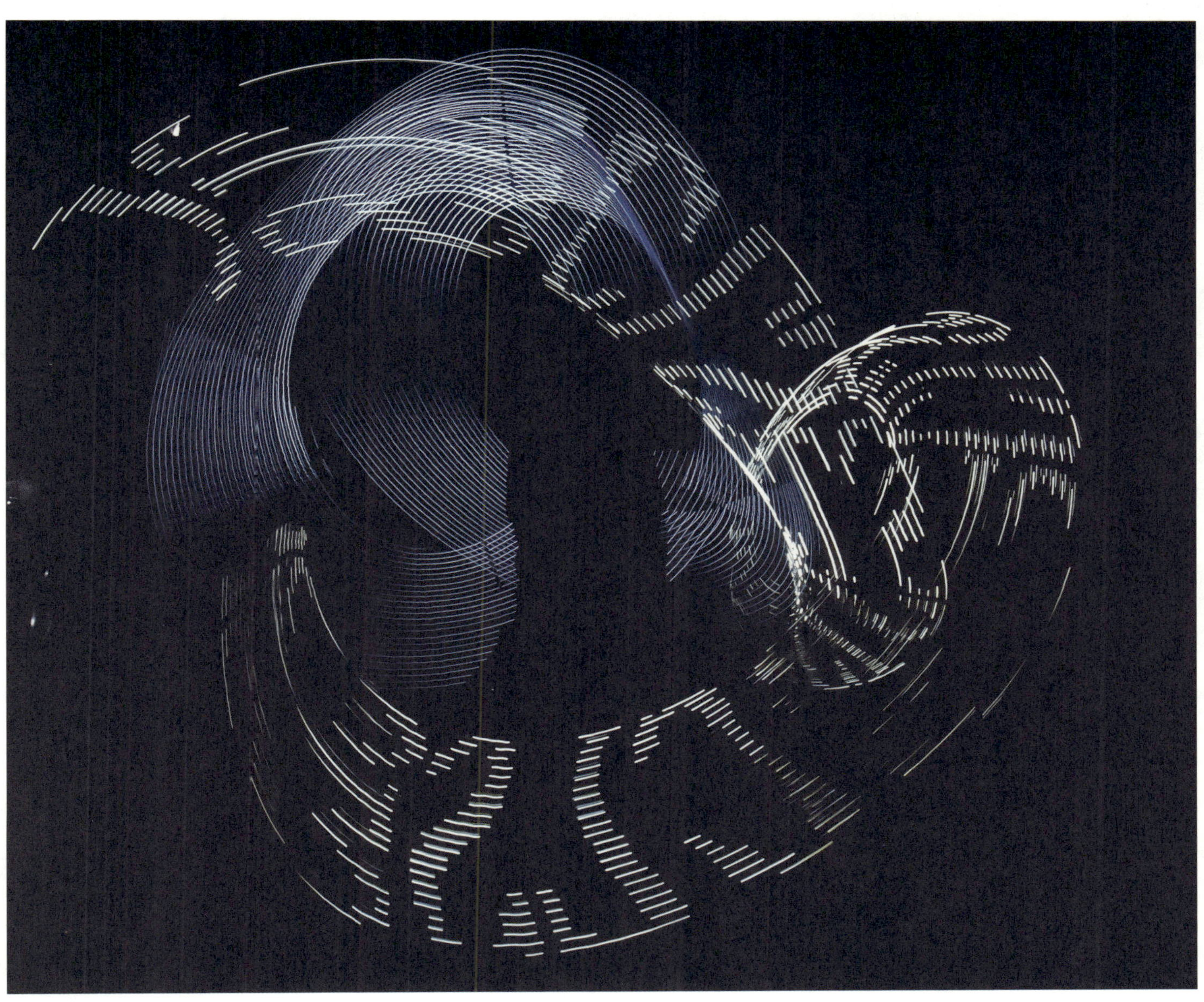

SHE'S_ ELECTR

Shortly after the Mercedes-Benz shoot, Ellie Goulding's video director approached Moritz Waldemeyer about a commission for the single, 'Lights.' With the 50 cameras still on loan this seemed like pure serendipity: they began shooting a week later. Moritz developed new, weapon-like props, inspired by the wide streams of graphics from the wushu sword and spear:

"THE SINGLE IS ABOUT A WOMAN TRYING TO FIND STRENGTH, SO IT WORKED WELL TO CAST ELLIE GOULDING AS A NEW AGE AMAZONIAN."

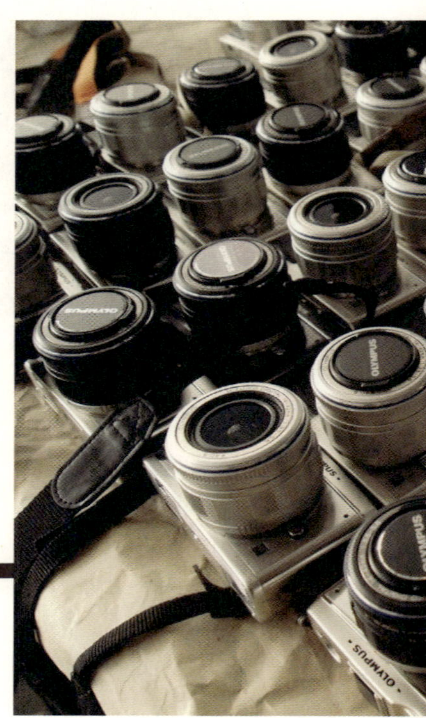

Moritz then designed graphics relating to the lyrics – a light bulb and a house – as well as graphics to express movement, blue lines and abstract dashes. Moritz also used a number of single-light source LED props in different colours to create constellation-like shapes around her, informed by Moritz's students' experiment at Boisbuchet. In the stills from the video we can see how Ellie Goulding's particular style of dance works with the props in a unique way. Through repeated, subtle movements, Ellie Goulding focuses on the pure act of painting with the lights as opposed to the disciplined attack of the martial artists. She produces whimsical visual magic of an entirely different atmosphere, highlighting the potential of the medium:

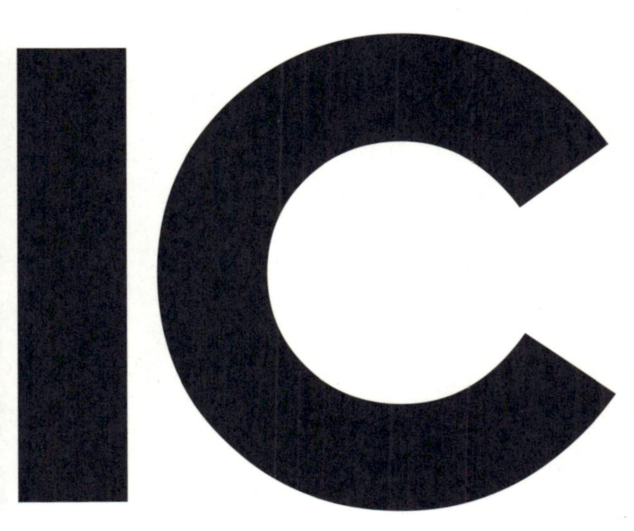

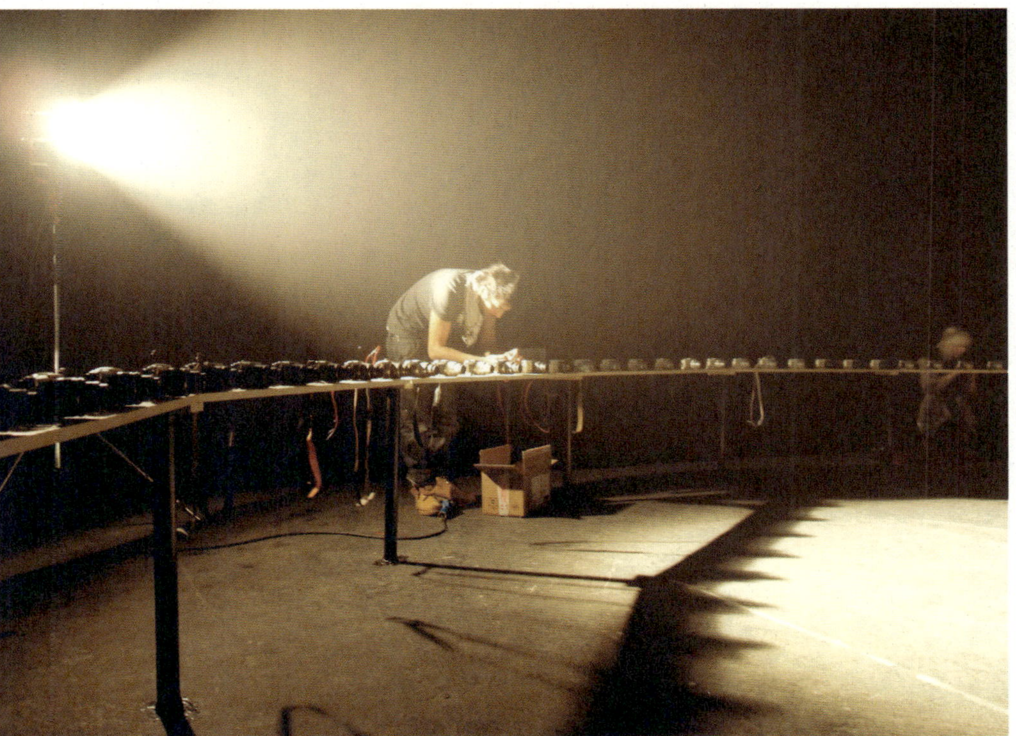

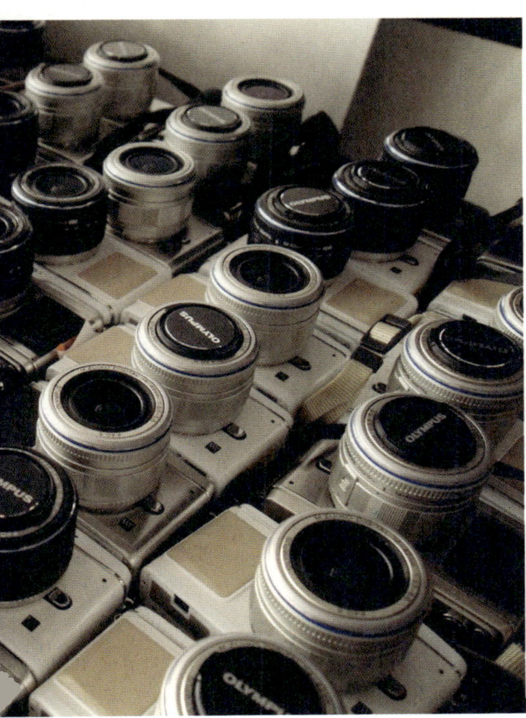

"THIS IS A VERY NEW TECHNOLOGY THAT HAS ONLY REALLY EMERGED OVER THE LAST TEN YEARS. BECAUSE OF THIS THERE ARE SO MANY POSSIBILITIES THAT JUST WERE NOT THERE BEFORE. ONLY NOW CAN YOU THINK ABOUT WHAT TO DO WITH THIS YOUNG, NEW, WONDERFUL TECHNOLOGY. THIS GIVES YOU REAL CREATIVE FREEDOM."

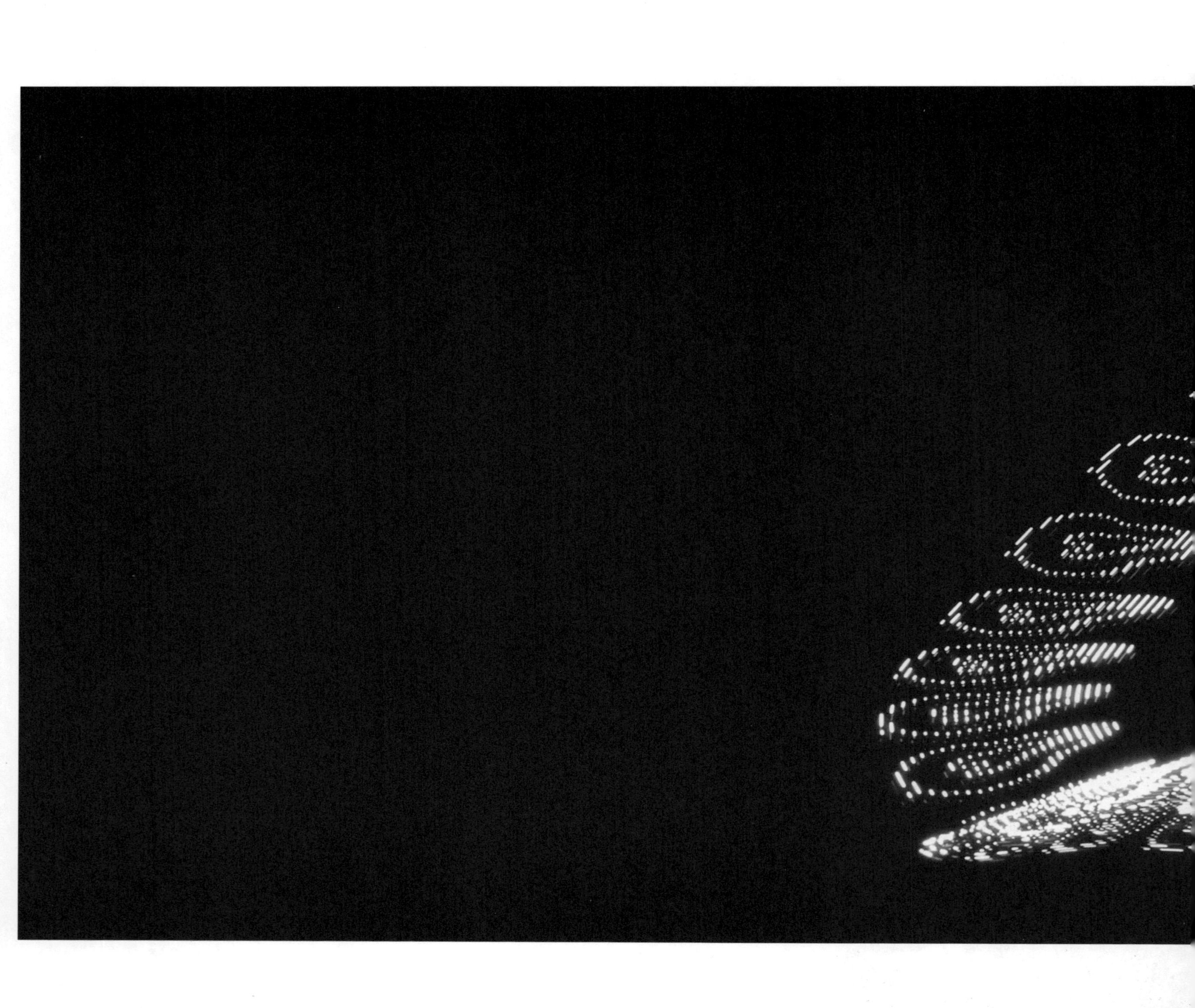

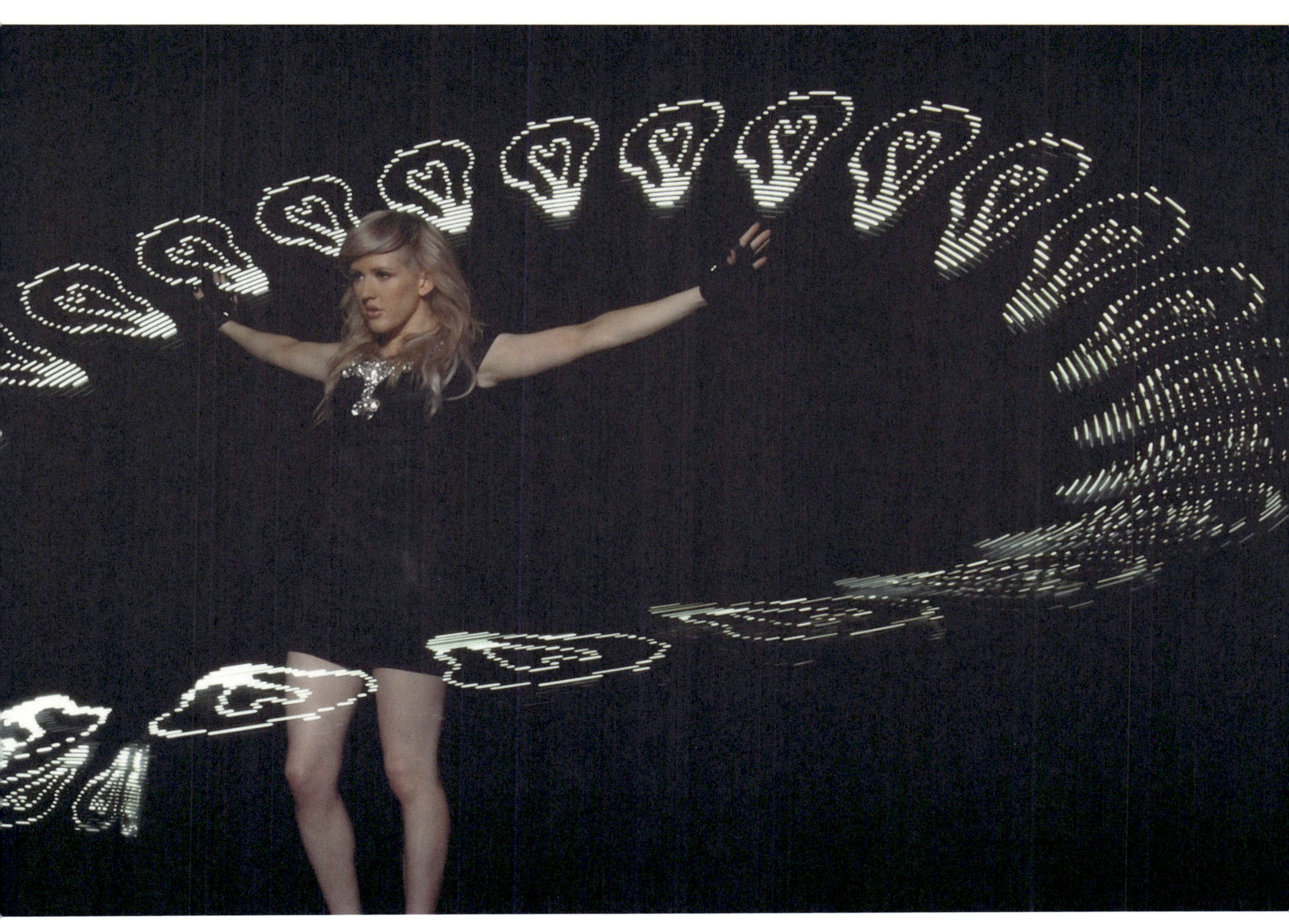

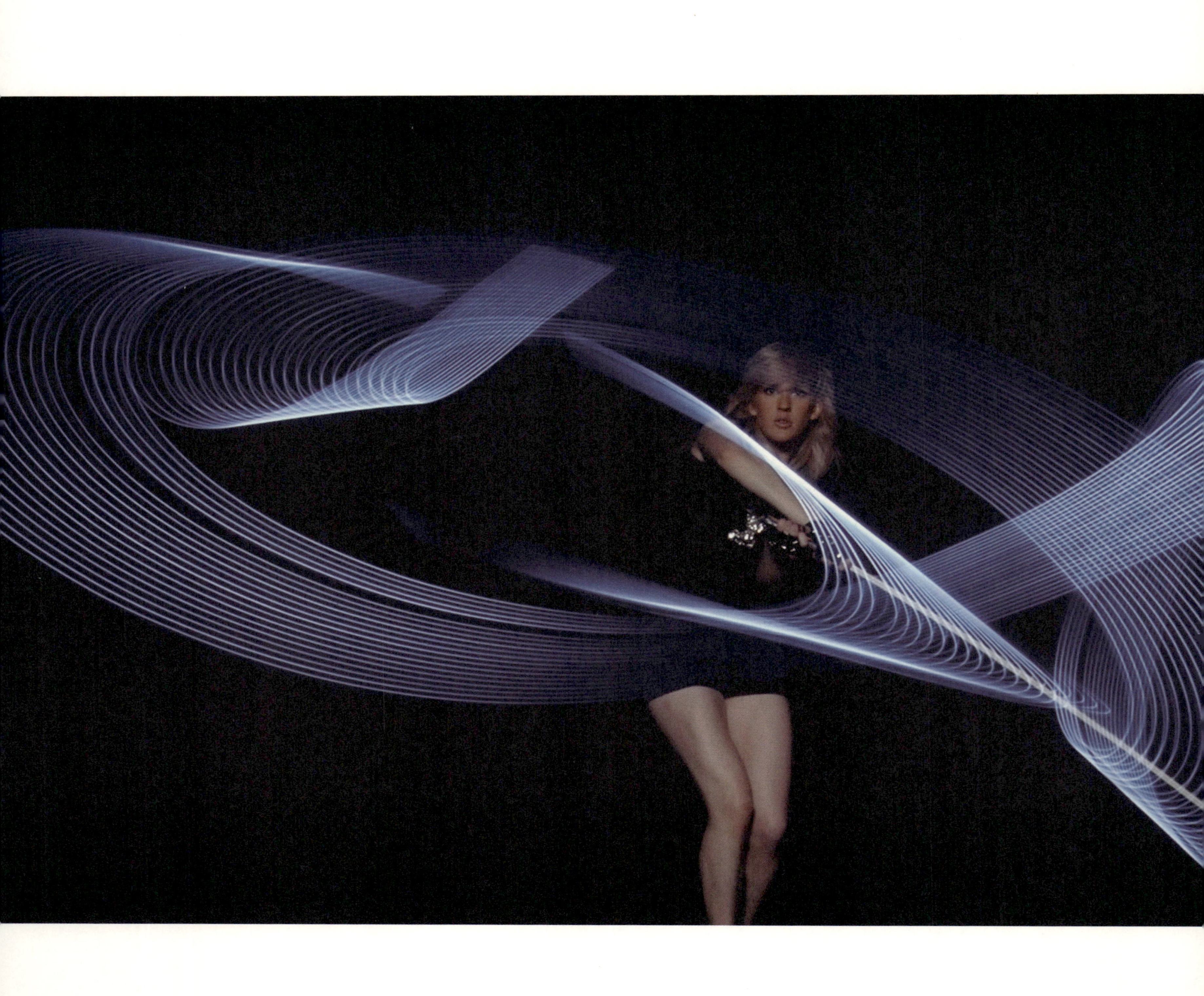

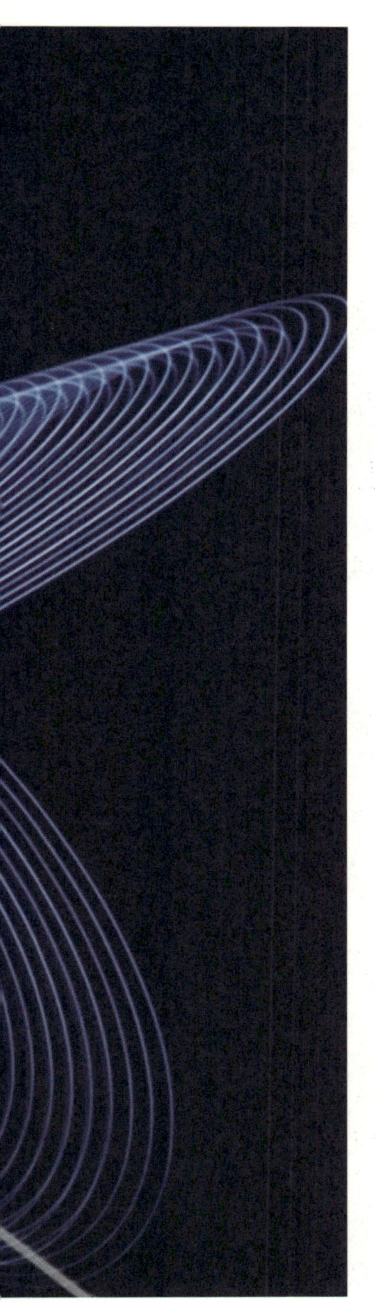

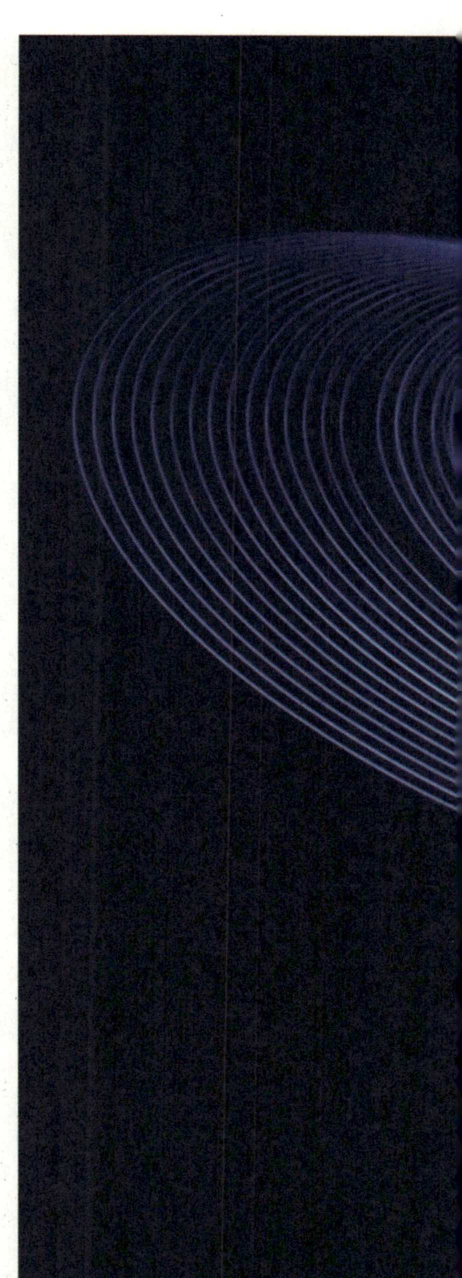

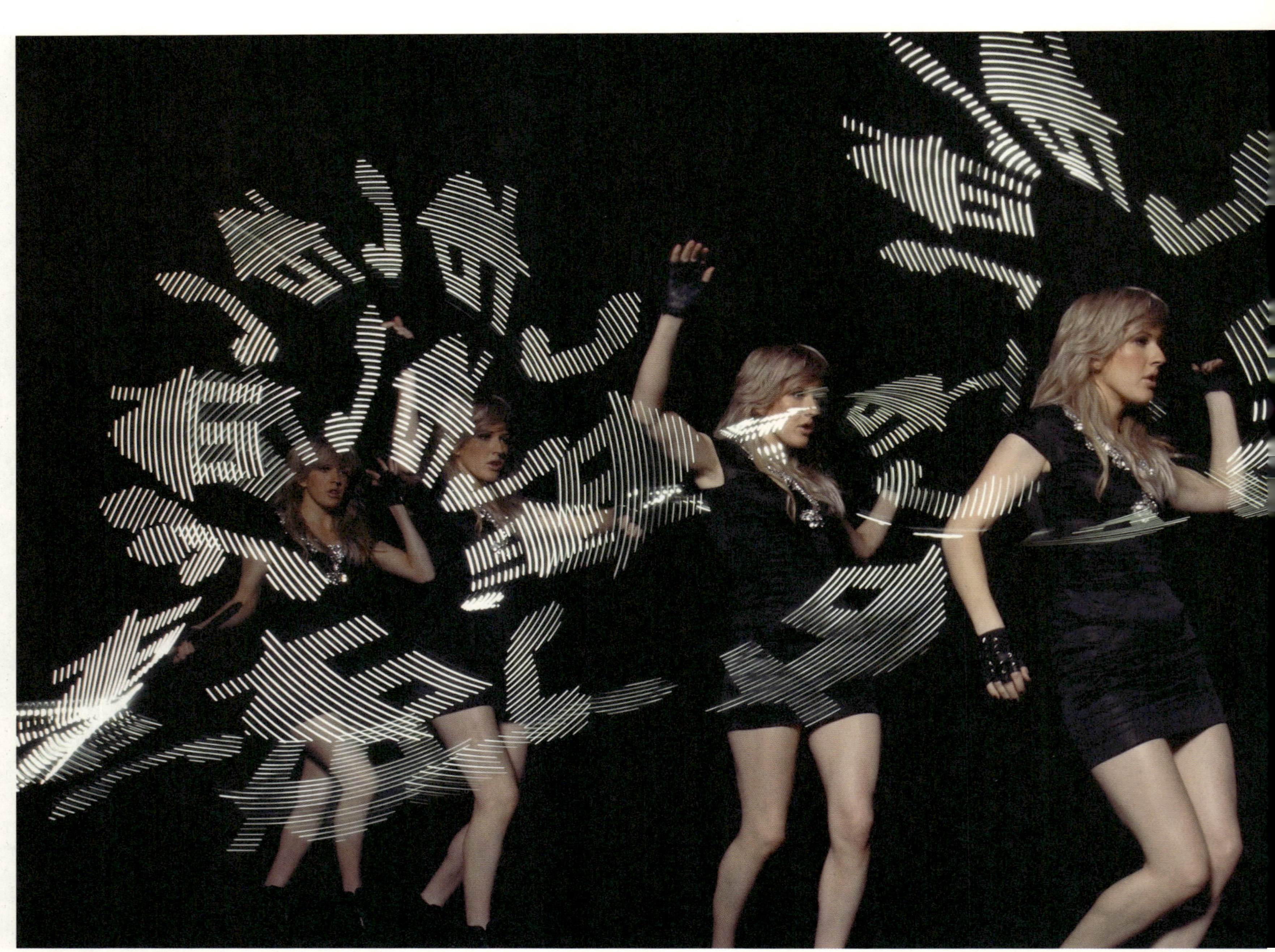

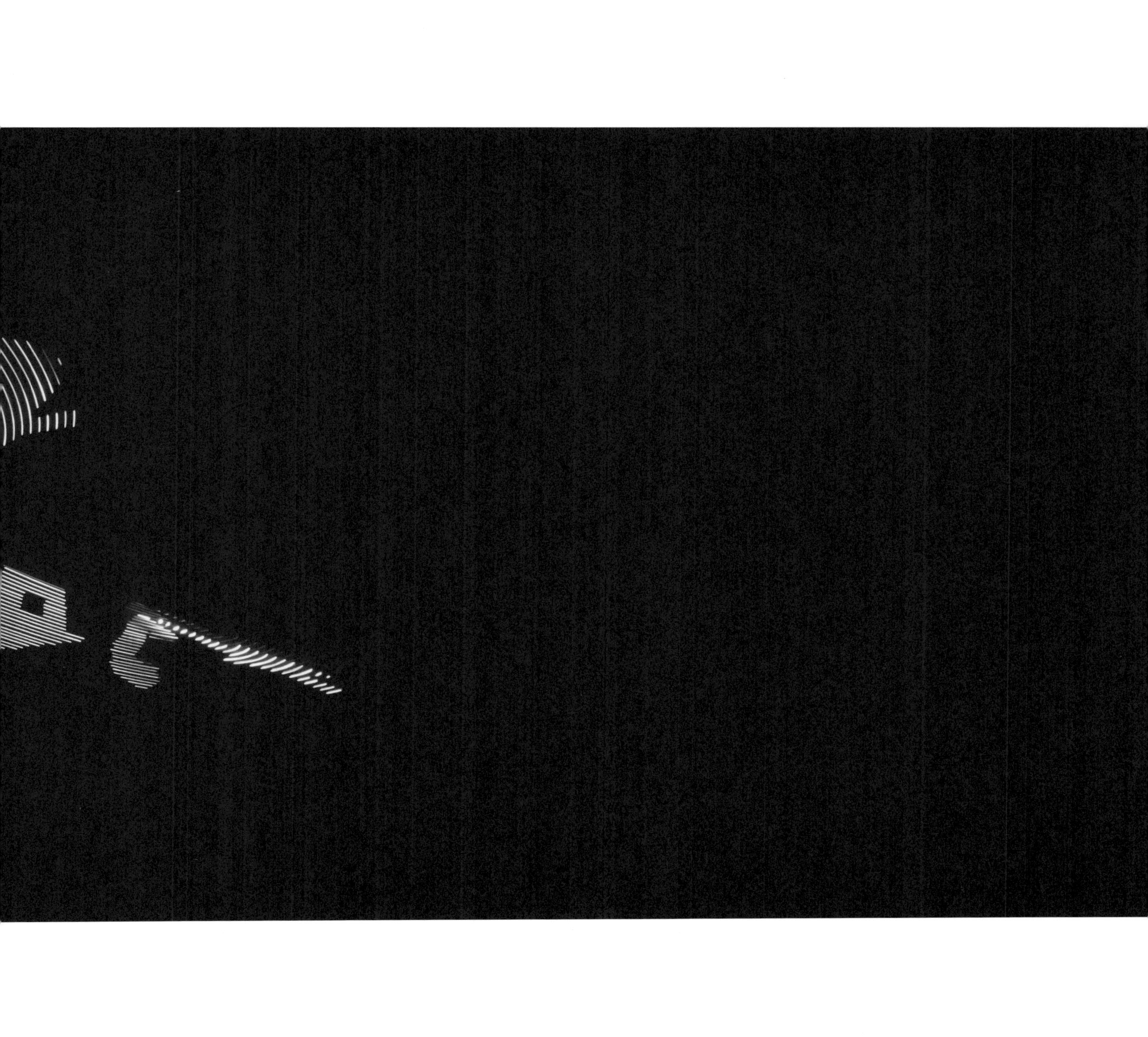

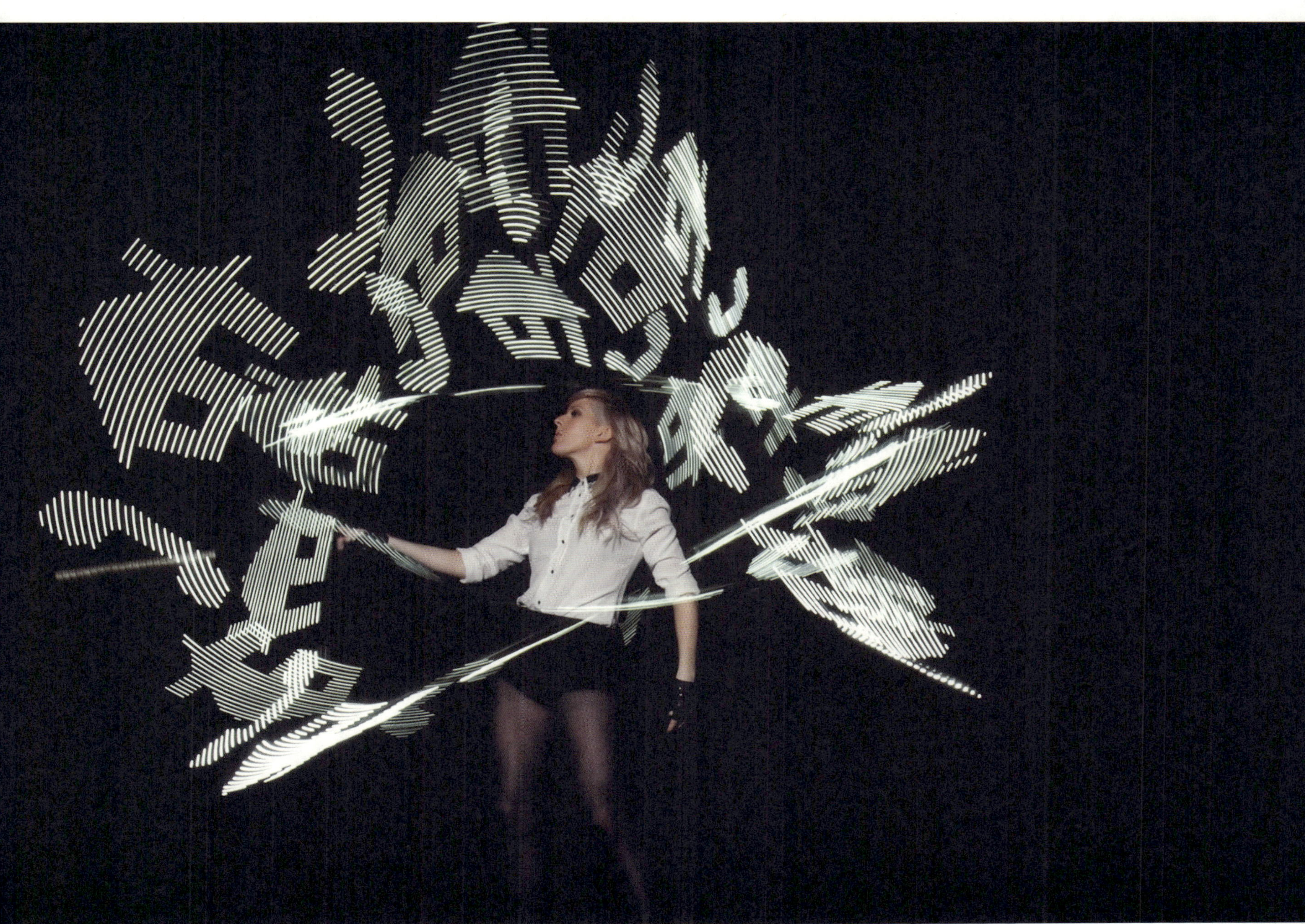

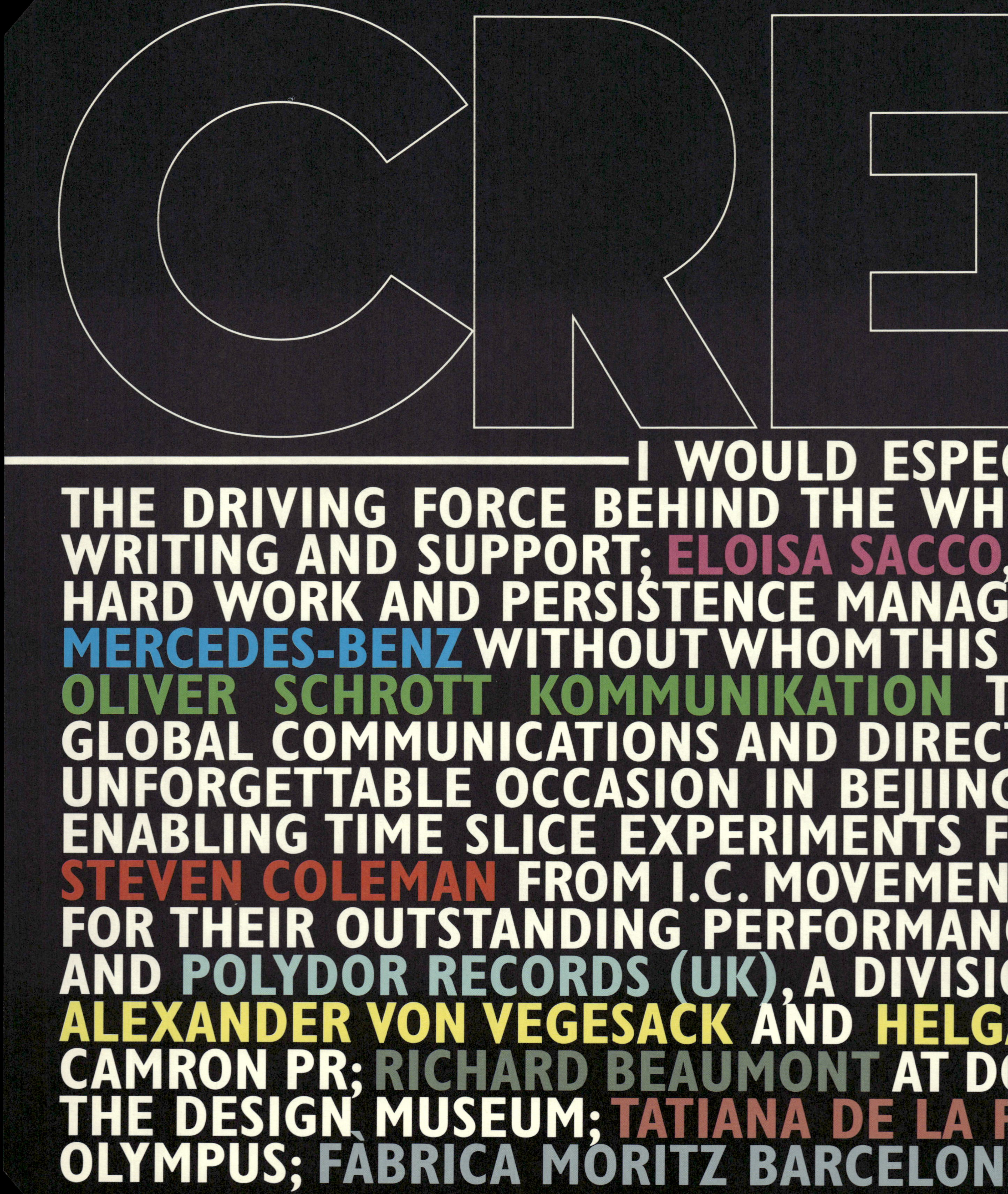

CRE

I WOULD ESPEC
THE DRIVING FORCE BEHIND THE WH
WRITING AND SUPPORT; ELOISA SACCO,
HARD WORK AND PERSISTENCE MANAG
MERCEDES-BENZ WITHOUT WHOM THIS
OLIVER SCHROTT KOMMUNIKATION T
GLOBAL COMMUNICATIONS AND DIRECT
UNFORGETTABLE OCCASION IN BEJIING
ENABLING TIME SLICE EXPERIMENTS F
STEVEN COLEMAN FROM I.C. MOVEMEN
FOR THEIR OUTSTANDING PERFORMANC
AND POLYDOR RECORDS (UK), A DIVISIO
ALEXANDER VON VEGESACK AND HELG
CAMRON PR; RICHARD BEAUMONT AT DO
THE DESIGN MUSEUM; TATIANA DE LA F
OLYMPUS; FÀBRICA MORITZ BARCELON

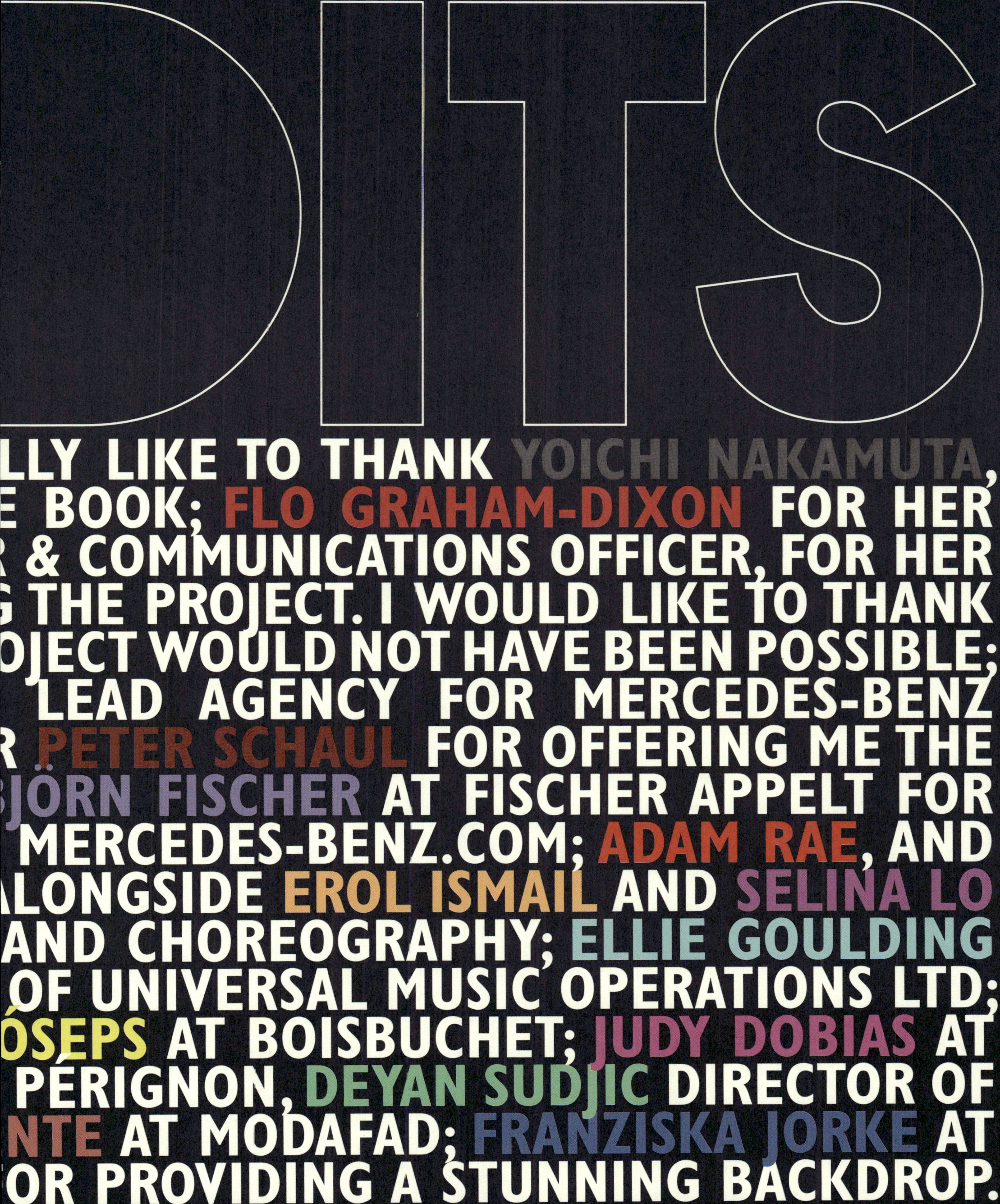
DITS
LLY LIKE TO THANK YOICHI NAKAMUTA,
E BOOK; FLO GRAHAM-DIXON FOR HER
R & COMMUNICATIONS OFFICER, FOR HER
G THE PROJECT. I WOULD LIKE TO THANK
OJECT WOULD NOT HAVE BEEN POSSIBLE;
LEAD AGENCY FOR MERCEDES-BENZ
R PETER SCHAUL FOR OFFERING ME THE
BJÖRN FISCHER AT FISCHER APPELT FOR
MERCEDES-BENZ.COM; ADAM RAE, AND
ALONGSIDE EROL ISMAIL AND SELINA LO
AND CHOREOGRAPHY; ELLIE GOULDING
OF UNIVERSAL MUSIC OPERATIONS LTD;
ÓSEPS AT BOISBUCHET; JUDY DOBIAS AT
PÉRIGNON, DEYAN SUDJIC DIRECTOR OF
NTE AT MODAFAD; FRANZISKA JORKE AT
OR PROVIDING A STUNNING BACKDROP.

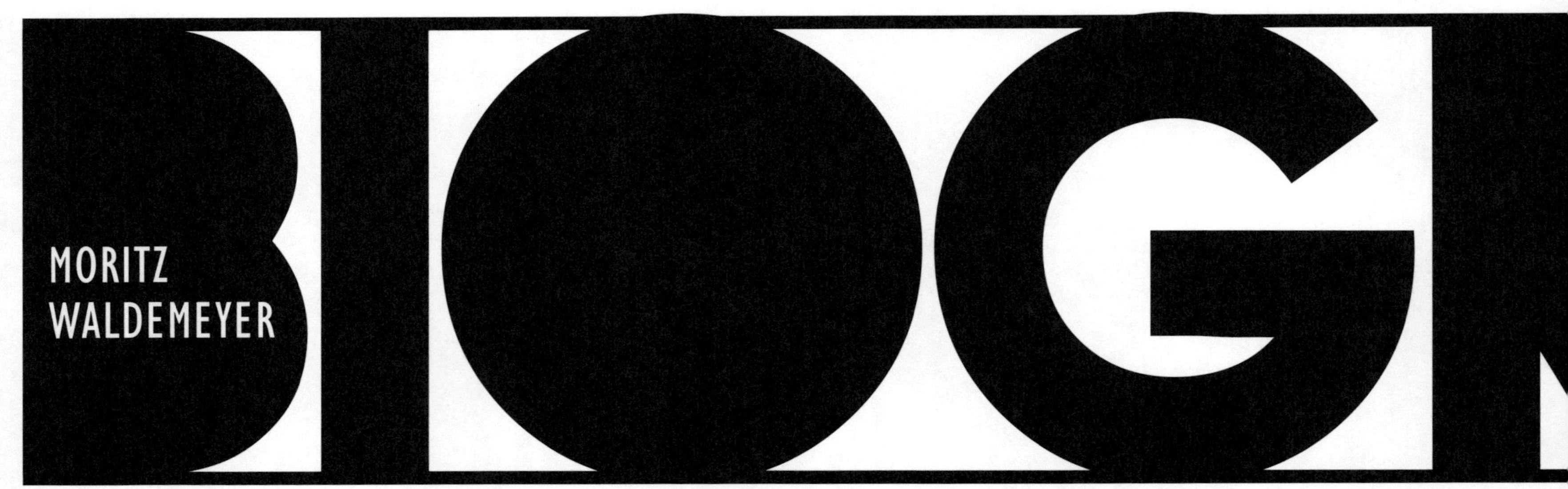

OVER THE PAST DECADE MORITZ WALDEMEYER HAS EARNED INTERNATIONAL RENOWN FOR HIS PIONEERING APPROACH TO LIGHTING DESIGN. HIS WORK HAS BROUGHT NEW APPLICATIONS OF LED AND LASER LIGHTING INTO THE ARENAS OF FASHION, DESIGN AND MUSIC PERFORMANCE, REVOLUTIONISING THEIR ARTISTIC VOCABULARY IN THE PROCESS.

RAISED IN HALLE, EAST GERMANY, MORITZ MOVED TO LONDON IN 1995 TO STUDY ENGINEERING AT KINGS COLLEGE. HE COMPLETED HIS MECHATRONICS MASTER'S DEGREE IN 2001 AND WENT ON TO COLLABORATE WITH SOME OF THE BIGGEST NAMES IN DESIGN, INCLUDING HUSSEIN CHALAYAN, ZAHA HADID, YVES BEHAR AND PHILIPPE STARCK.

MORITZ WALDEMEYER ALSO HAS A STRONG INDEPENDENT AND COMMERCIAL PORTFOLIO THAT ILLUMINATES THE GREY AREA BETWEEN TECHNOLOGY AND CREATIVE INGENUITY. IN 2012 HE BEGAN WORK WITH INGO MAURER ON A SERIES OF INNOVATIVE LIGHTING DESIGNS, UNVEILING THE INSTALLATION 'CANDLE IN THE WIND' AT MILAN DESIGN WEEK. HIS MORE RECENT EXPANSION INTO THE MUSIC INDUSTRY HAS BORNE FRUITFUL COLLABORATIONS WITH U2, RIHANNA, TAKE THAT AND KYLIE MINOGUE. MOST RECENTLY, MORITZ ENGINEERED LED-EMBEDDED CARNIVAL COSTUMES FOR THE OLYMPIC HANDOVER CEREMONY, ESTIMATED TO BE VIEWED BY FOUR BILLION PEOPLE WORLDWIDE.

APHY

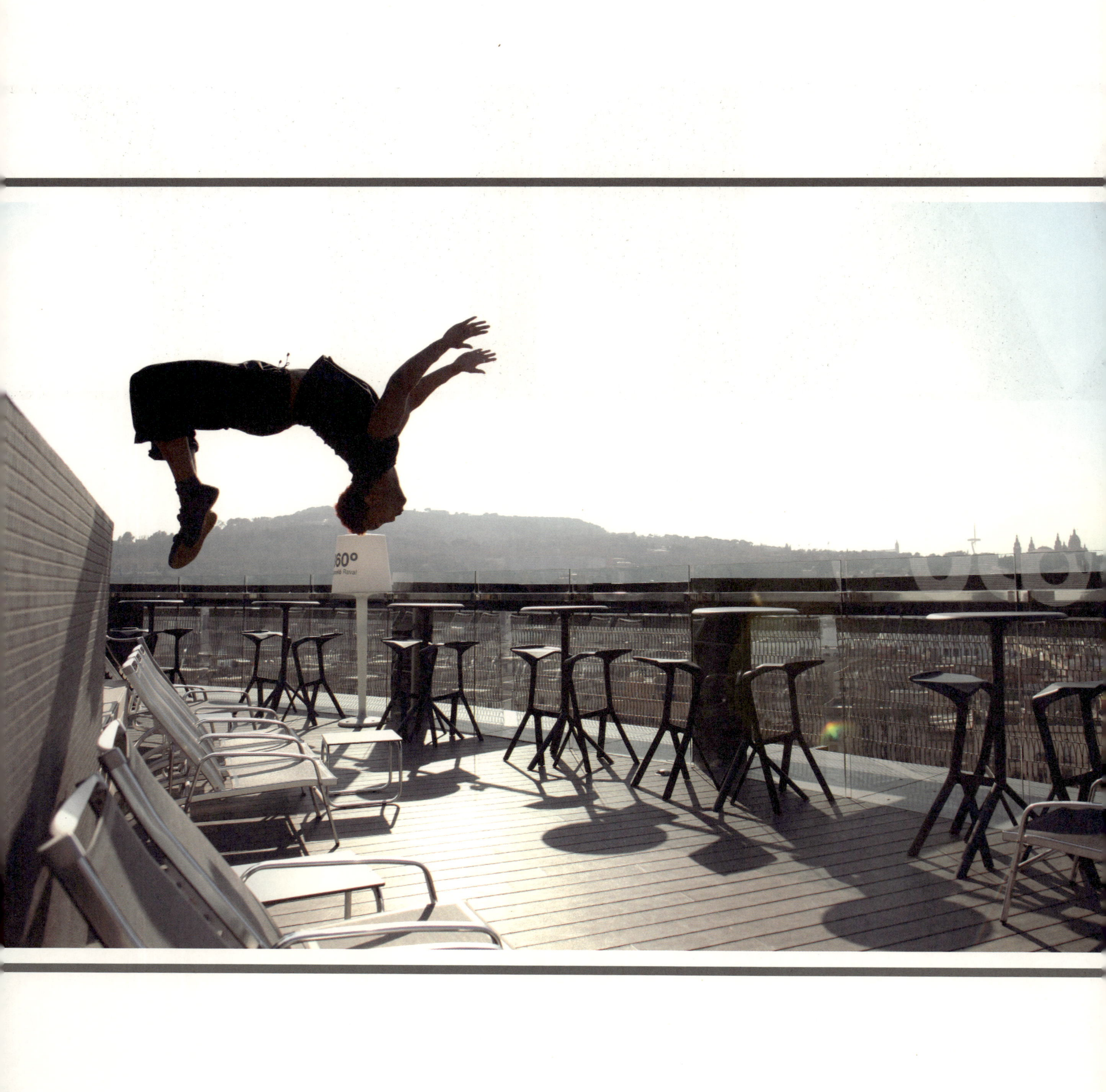
60°
Raval

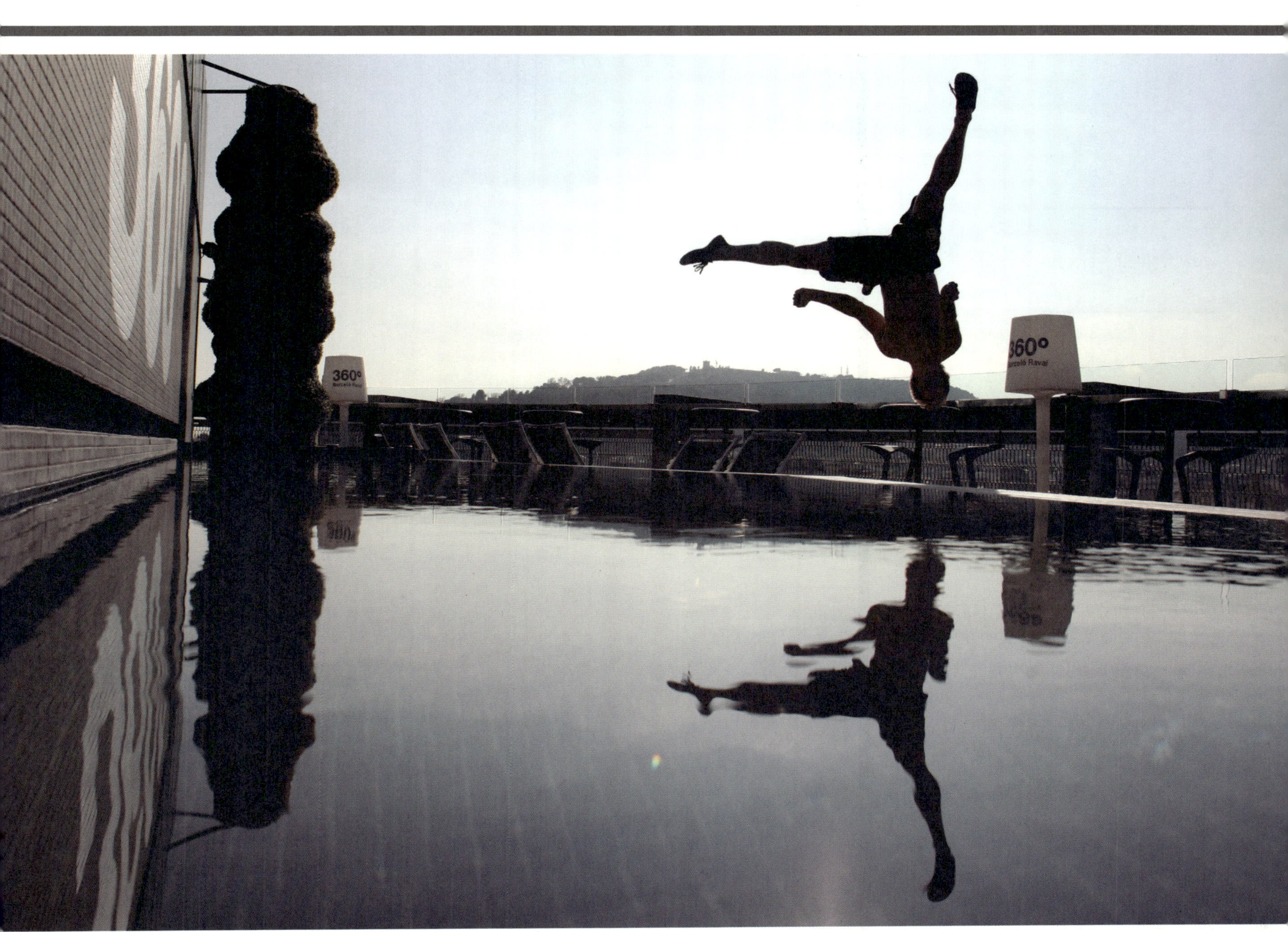
360°
360°
Raval

www.waldemeyer.com

THE PATH OF THE SWORD

is published by
CLEAR EDITION INC.
2/F, 7-18-8 Roppongi,
Minato-ku,Tokyo 106-0032 Japan
contact@clearedition.jp
website: www.clearedition.jp

ISBN 978-4-9904112-4-4

is printed by
Also Dominie Pte Ltd.
T: +65 6273 0755
www.dominie.com.sg

is designed by
STUDIO Am
amalinelim@gmail.com